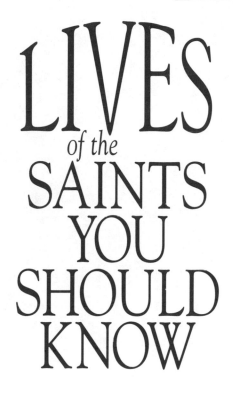

LIVES
of the
SAINTS
YOU
SHOULD
KNOW

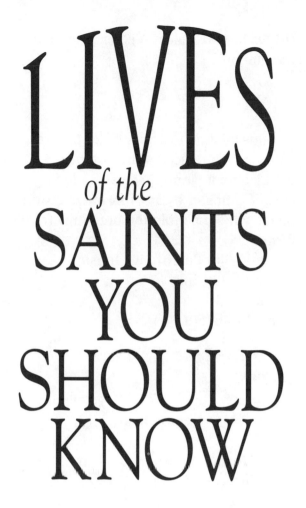

LIVES
of the
SAINTS
YOU
SHOULD
KNOW

MARGARET & MATTHEW BUNSON

Our Sunday Visitor Publishing Division
Our Sunday Visitor, Inc.
Huntington, Indiana 46750

Our Sunday Visitor Publishing Division
Our Sunday Visitor, Inc.
200 Noll Plaza
Huntington, IN 46750

ISBN: 0-87973-576-7
LCCN: 94-67356

PRINTED IN THE UNITED STATES OF AMERICA

Cover design by Monica Watts
Illustrations by Margaret Bunson

576-7

Contents

I saw a great multitude
which no man could number,
of all nations, and tribes,
and peoples, and tongues,
standing before the throne
and in sight of the Lamb,
clothed with white robes
and palms in their hands.

Little Chapter
Feast of All Saints

Foreword

Who Are Saints?

The term "saint" comes from the Latin word *sanctus*, meaning something holy or consecrated. Stephen, the first martyr, who was stoned to death for the faith, was declared a saint sometime around the year A.D. 35, so the idea of honoring holy men and women and venerating (showing great respect to) their relics is not an invention of the modern world.

Saints are men and women who have been "raised to the altars of the Church." This means that they have been recognized as the Friends of God who intercede for (speak on behalf of) all living people before the Throne of God. They also protect the men and women on earth from evils and, in some cases, bring about miracles.

The early martyrs of the Church were normally given the title "Venerable" at their deaths. Others such as apostles, missionaries, and confessors — those who witnessed for Christ — were also venerated. Their feast days date back to the second century. Most of these feast days are anniversaries of the days on which these men and women died, for their physical deaths only opened the door to the eternal joys waiting for such Friends of God.

Of course, some areas of the world had particular traditions or legends concerning the holy men and women of their areas. Many of these men and women were raised to high honors without any true historical facts to back up the legends; their popularity was the only thing necessary. In order to make things right, Pope Innocent III (A.D. 1199-1216) began a process for naming saints and raising such individuals to high honors. The modern process of determining the truth of claims of sanctity made on behalf of men and women — called *canonization* — began in A.D. 1634.

Three separate terms are used today to rank the Friends of God throughout the Church:

• The first, "Venerable," is a title given to men and women considered possible candidates for canonization. Some really remarkable individuals have the title "Venerable" and some date to ancient eras. Their "Causes" — the *process* leading to canonization — were started but then did not proceed. This does not mean that these men and women were not holy, but rather that the steps necessary for canonization were not completed for one reason or another.

• The term "Blessed" is given to men and women who have been "Beatified" by the Church. Beatification is the declaration made by the pope that a man or woman has been proven to have lived virtuously and to have merited heaven's reward. Such individuals are named as worthy of veneration only in their homelands or in the houses of their religious orders.

• The term "Saint" comes with the last step of canonization. This is the official seal of approval by the Church. Veneration of the men and women canonized (declared) as saints is ordered throughout the whole Church. Remember that the saints are venerated (honored) and looked upon as eternal friends. They are not adored. Adoration is reserved only for Almighty God.

The saints — the Friends of God — are also involved in another aspect of Catholic life, one mentioned in the Apostles' Creed. They are part of the "Communion of Saints" — that is, the spiritual connection between the saints in heaven, the souls in purgatory, and the men and women still living on earth. This is a union that helps people still working toward their own salvation, by offering them graces and the inspiration to perform good works. Human beings still in the world can imitate the saints and ask their aid; the saints also can pray for the souls in purgatory.

The saints serve as patrons and protectors of certain places or people. Their careers during their own earthly lifetimes, their types of martyrdom, or some particular event in their lives have been translated into special roles on earth. Patron saints have always been popular, with some types of veneration (called cults) dating back to ancient times.

Introduction

The word "saint" scares some people, and makes others uneasy. This is not exactly an age when holiness is given media coverage or praised around the world. You don't see saints on the cover of *Sports Illustrated*! There are, of course, men and women, such as Mother Teresa of Calcutta, whose goodness shines through the everyday blur of news and events, but the idea of being saintly is not taught to many young people anymore, and for this reason there is a great deal of confusion about saints as individuals.

People tend to forget that the saints honored by the Church were men and women who lived on earth just like other human beings. Each one was different, and each offers a fascinating and sometimes exciting adventure for those who take the time to learn about them.

Young people of today may think that saints are peculiar beings who hide in dark corners, where they pray and moan about the wicked ways of the world. Some believe that saints are always kind, patient, and long-suffering. One opinion remains popular today, especially among young people: saints make everyone around them look bad.

The saints have been, and always will be, ordinary men and women who managed somehow to make extraordinary choices every day of their lives, especially when God asked them to accomplish some particular purpose. Not all of them died as martyrs for the faith, mainly because they lived in times when the Church no longer faced such terrible trials or persecutions. Some were not very patient or long-suffering in their dealings with their fellow humans, particularly when they were defending the weak and the poor. A few of them, in fact, drove everyone around them crazy because they would not play it safe or conform to the demands of the world.

When people speak of the "universality" of the Church —
the fact that the faith has attracted men and women from all
nations and from all walks of life — the saints are good
examples. They have lived in every era of the Christian age, and
their personalities were shaped by many cultures and by many
different experiences. These men and women, products of their
own national or local traditions, reach past the normal things in
life to embrace God. Their adventures were woven out of their
particular time, out of their responses to the faith, and their
relationships with other people. Each one served God and his or
her fellow human beings; but the saints shared as well a single
joyous capacity to love God, to know Him, and to imitate His
Son, the Christ.

Perhaps the most startling aspect of saints and their lives is
the simple fact that goodness comes in so many beautiful and
exciting packages. Evil is boring, whether the modern world
will admit that fact or not. Evil has to be dressed up in slogans,
in a new beat, in images that will make it appear the "in" thing
to do, really "fun." People who live in the so-called "fast lane,"
a lifestyle of empty pleasures and irresponsible behavior,
always have to find new ways of keeping themselves amused or
excited. Goodness, on the other hand, comes in many forms and
shades: in small kindnesses, in soothing words, in
compassionate care, in remembering and valuing others for
their worth, even in the surrendering of one's life to keep others
free or secure.

Goodness shines through the world on its own, and it never
needs advertising or slogans to make it glisten and attract
others. Every single person alive has met at least one good
person along the way, received one gentle pat of
encouragement, one kind word, a sign of compassion or
sympathy, or maybe was lent a willing ear when things looked
really bad. Those who march against evil, perhaps by standing
up in endless committee hearings to fight for those unable to
defend themselves, perhaps by taking a stand on a school

playground to stop the bullying of another student, are also good people. They show the world that goodness is not hidden in a dark closet, but is rather prayer in action.

The saints are special human beings, called by God to complete special jobs during their lives. They take goodness one step beyond the normal limits, achieving lasting monuments to the faith. The saints included in this book will demonstrate goodness taken to its very heights, but the stories of these men and women will not be alike in their historical settings or in the details of their adventures.

The people discussed here are unique, because in being saints they assumed the ways of Christ, and in doing that they became themselves to the fullest degree, using all of their skills and energies to serve God and to make the world a better place for the generations to follow upon the earth.

Margaret and Matthew Bunson

Agatha

Chapter 1

Agatha

Agatha was one of the most highly revered and honored martyrs of the Church during the Roman era. We don't know much about her birth and life, but it is known that Agatha was a member of a noble family belonging to the class called "patricians." The patrician class in Rome was considered important because these nobles had inherited power, good standing in the community because of their name, and wealth that had been gathered and safeguarded over the decades. When the patricians showed an interest in Christianity, they were feared by the Roman authorities as potential troublemakers. Because of the possibilities of such conversions to the Church, when patricians became Christians they were punished quickly and publicly.

Jesus had taught that all men and women were the sons and daughters of God. That meant that the slaves and commoners of Rome and its provinces were equal to Caesar in God's eyes, an idea that did not appeal to those in power at the time. Certainly, no emperor was thrilled to hear that kind of talk, not while he was on the throne! Such a belief could turn Rome upside down, especially if the patricians decided that Jesus' words were true. Equality could bring a lot of trouble to the empire and to the established order of things.

There was no real way to stop the spread of Christianity, and by the end of the second century the Romans knew it, being people who faced up to the facts of life. They could, however, with care and vigilance, keep the faith centered in the ranks of the slaves and commoners, who were not powerful in the Roman world. Slaves and commoners became Christians even in the earliest days, but the higher ranking Romans seldom paid any attention. If the lower classes felt better having such a belief, that was fine with the authorities and the nobles, who did not like the idea of associating with the lower classes just to say a few prayers. Let the slaves and commoners join the faith, as long as they didn't try to convert anyone important or make changes in the way the empire operated.

The patricians, on the other hand, counted the founding fathers of Rome as their ancestors and had the power to change the empire if they expressed their dissatisfaction with the way the government authorities conducted affairs. For this reason, the authorities were very careful to watch for Christians among the noble families. They viewed these converts to the faith as traitors — not only to Rome, but to their own noble class.

The first Christian nobles in the Roman Empire had to be brave and cherish the gift of the faith because of this watchfulness, and because of the prejudice against the growing Church. Many patricians believed that Christians were low-lifes, belonging to an alien culture, and bent on making trouble for decent folk. They listened to the rumors spread about the Christians and declared the faith unfit for any Roman. While the rumors and prejudice stopped some Romans from accepting Christianity, the authorities knew that there were always a few who would risk everything once they had made up their mind. For this reason they asked that anyone among the patrician clans be reported if he or she became a Christian. Persecutions took place in many imperial eras, especially during the reign of Emperor Decius, who felt obligated to murder as many Christians as he could lay his hands on. Agatha was a victim of just such a persecution in Catania, Sicily, sometime around A.D. 250-253, over 1,700 years ago.

Now, no one dies for an *opinion*! No sane person rushes to martyrdom because he or she *sort of feels* a certain way or *thinks* that something is *probably* true. A person is willing to suffer and die only when he or she *knows* the truth. People don't offer themselves to torturers or executioners for fun, especially not to the cruel thugs who waited in the ancient Roman dungeons.

A young woman named Agatha, of a patrician family, met a Roman Senator named Quintianus, who promptly fell in love with her. The fact that Agatha was young didn't bother him, as many Roman middle-aged men married teenage girls so that they could train them from the beginning of the marriage. Quintianus was ambitious, and having a beautiful patrician wife would help his career. Agatha, however, refused his proposal of marriage, which caught Quintianus off guard and made him angry.

Quintianus believed that Agatha possibly had a boyfriend already, and decided to have his henchmen follow her so that he could discover his rival and then get rid of him somehow. He was used to getting his way and hated anyone who denied him what he wanted.

Within days his men reported that Agatha was not meeting a young man but rather was attending Christian meetings. Quintianus, seeing an opportunity to take revenge upon Agatha and to make a name for himself at the same time, raced to the office of the local governor to announce that his "true love" was a rotten Christian, a traitor to her noble class and to Rome.

The governor, probably horrified by the charge and by the fact that Quintianus had made such an awful accusation against a noble person, had to act because that was the law. Quintianus was playing the role of a patriot by telling everyone that he was a hero who had fallen under Agatha's evil spell but had saved himself and was now about to save the empire. As a Senator he had powerful friends and political allies. If the governor didn't give Quintianus his revenge by punishing Agatha, Quintianus would destroy the governor along with the young Christian.

No one knows what Agatha's family members did when they heard the news. Most of them probably stood beside Quintianus in denouncing the girl. After all, their rank and their fortunes could be swept away if the whole family was accused of Christianity. Someone in the family or in the governor's office, however, finally came up with a compromise to keep Agatha out of the hands of the Roman torturers. It was agreed that she could save herself by renouncing Christ and the Church. Since she was young and a patrician, she could accuse others of leading her astray, and be believed. The accused would be tortured to death, but Agatha would be free and available to be given to Quintianus in marriage. Having saved her from torture, of course, Quintianus would never have let Agatha forget his generosity.

But Agatha blamed no one and did not renounce Christ or the Church before the government magistrates. With joy she confirmed publicly that she was a Christian. That announcement shocked everyone in the governor's court, naturally. Her happy confession of faith resulted in her being thrown into the dungeons as a common criminal. All of her privileges of rank disappeared and she was just another Christian who would be tortured and slain by the professional killers.

The men who worked in these terrible pits of agony were probably shocked at receiving such a delicate prisoner. They began to beat her, cursing her as they used the lash, and then they cut off parts of her body. These wounds were designed to cause her pain and bring her near death but not to kill her. The torturers in the Roman dungeons were supposed to make the pain last as long as possible.

Returned to her cell, Agatha was thrown into a corner, where rats and mice crawled about, biting her and chattering. That night, however, Agatha received a vision of Saint Peter, and she was restored to perfect health, with no scars, as all the terrible lashes and wounds disappeared. When the magistrate's men arrived the next morning to haul her before the governor, they were struck dumb by her loveliness and by her good health. No doubt, one or two of her tormenters suffered their own grisly fates, after trying to explain to the governor that they really had mutilated her young body. Their explanations, of course, would not have convinced anyone, because few Roman officials would believe that Saint Peter, who had been crucified on Vatican Hill centuries before, had walked into the dungeon and healed the patrician maiden.

The only thing that the Romans could do was to begin the tortures all over again. This time the henchmen in the dungeons did not care if she lived through the lashings and burnings. Agatha died at their hands, never renouncing Christ or the Church, and leaving a stunned patrician class to ponder her fate and her Christianity. In time, when the Church converted thousands and made Rome its own holy city, Agatha was canonized and given February 5 as her feast day each year. She is one of the most highly revered virgin martyrs, and she is invoked (or called upon) to keep the local populations safe from eruptions of Mt. Etna, the ferocious volcano in Italy. Within the Universal Church, Agatha is the patroness of nursing.

Thomas Becket

Chapter 2

Thomas Becket

Sometimes saints do not start out being "Friends of God." There are some men and women now honored by the Church who took a "long road" to understanding the world and the Church in their lives, and in the lives of other people. Actually, this sort of beginning makes such saints appealing. Because we can see they were as confused and scared as everyone else, it makes them easier to understand and appreciate.

Just such a person was a man named Thomas à Beckct, as the Normans called him in merry old England. Born in London in 1118, he had a political career during the reign of King Henry II, who was the father of future kings Richard the Lion-Hearted and Black Prince John. Their mother was the Queen, famed Eleanor of Aquitaine. This was the age when Robin Hood and his archers roamed Nottingham Forest, robbing the rich and giving to the poor.

Thomas Becket was a close friend and companion of Henry II, despite the fact that he had studied in the seminary and had received the "minor orders," which meant that he had been ordained a deacon and an archdeacon (one step below the priesthood). Thomas Becket used to spend time with the king in the local taverns in the evenings, or go out in the hunting areas. The use of these areas was restricted to the upper classes; the poor villagers, who needed the meat of the wild animals kept in the preserves, could not trespass into the woods. If they hunted there they were called poachers, and faced terrible punishments.

When King Henry II was not busy drinking and playing

jokes on his courtiers, he spent his time waging war on the Church in England. Henry was always desperate for money, and he kept looking at the Church's buildings and lands, trying to figure out some scheme by which he could take control of the property and then sell it. Thomas Becket, always at his side, thought up several plans, some of which proved rather successful, and he aided the king in giving the English bishops troubles. Because he was one of the few individuals that King Henry could trust, Becket was made the Chancellor of England. He was also brighter than most at the time.

Now the bishops were not thrilled by Thomas's lifestyle and they were even less thrilled by his clever schemes for taking away their properties and their rights. To begin with, Thomas was a man of culture, a rarity in those days. Some records claim that he introduced the British court to the use of the fork. Although the upper classes in other European countries had knives and forks, it appears that the English still used their fingers to eat. Some people even said that the fork was the "devil's tool," something to be avoided by decent folk.

Thomas liked poetry, music, and dancing, and he gave exciting parties at his beautiful estates. The Chancellors of England had many mansions, as well as titles and money. King Henry kept borrowing Thomas's money, but repaid him with more lands and more fancy titles. Certainly, Thomas's brains were the best weapon that Henry had against the ruthless barons of England, who were sturdy men with their own lands and armies who would have liked to see the monarchy fall.

During King Henry's time, however, the barons were unable to force him to do anything. The king had Thomas's brains and the strong arms of several knights who liked to settle arguments by breaking heads. Life went on smoothly for the king, although the English bishops had to walk carefully and prayerfully, because Henry was always there reaching out his greedy hands.

Then the office of Archbishop of Canterbury became vacant. Every nation has what is called the "Primal See," the original Church office that serves as the headquarters for the country. Canterbury was the Primal See in England, and whoever ruled from there could control the ongoing affairs of the Church and England, ruled by Henry II. The king decided to astound and confound his enemies by naming Thomas Becket as Archbishop of Canterbury. He knew that the other bishops of England would be shocked at the thought of such a man heading the Church in the isles. To King Henry's amazement, however, Thomas Becket pleaded to be spared the appointment.

Thomas, for all his wild ways, knew himself and his own nature. He was a man who did not commit easily to a cause or to a person, but once he made that choice, he did not allow anything or anyone to stand in his way of fulfilling the role expected of him. He begged King Henry to leave him alone, to be content with what he was doing for the monarchy. Henry only laughed, because he knew he could eliminate all opposition if the Church was in the hands of a trusted ally. So Thomas Becket was ordained a priest and consecrated the Archbishop of Canterbury, the defender of the Church in Britain.

King Henry noticed a change in Thomas instantly. Thomas began to sell his mansions and properties, including his golden forks, and gave the money to the poor. He fed hundreds who came to Canterbury for help. He slept very little, kneeling before the crucifix in his room, and wearing a "hair shirt," a rough, scratchy undergarment that made him uncomfortable but was worn as an act of penitence at the time.

Thomas Becket, now ordained and given the task of shepherding the Church through dangerous political times, was showing the "grace of office." God had chosen him, and he was providing Thomas with the joys and the courage to stand firm in defense of the faith. Actually, Thomas became such a saintly man that King Henry found himself without a friend in his nightly tours of the local taverns. The new Archbishop of

Canterbury did not run around having fun and playing jokes on people. He prayed, did penance, and took care of the needs of the Church. He also took pity on the poor and the wretched and gave them everything they needed.

His action did not win him friends among the English bishops. First of all, they did not trust his new displays of holiness. It was hard for them to believe that Thomas did not have some grand scheme up his sleeve, a plot to give Henry II more power and wealth. The bishops were rather cold-hearted and worldly compared to this crazy man who ran around giving away everything that he possessed. His humility made him suspect as far as the other bishops were concerned. They had expected he would put on airs and strut around in his fancy robes. Instead he worked side by side with the monks at Canterbury and allowed the poor to come to see him without an appointment. Thomas was also known to laugh a great deal, to sing and smile, which did not make him look at all like someone who had just recently been given such a high office.

Henry II fretted and raved until a series of events took place that brought matters to a head between him and Thomas. For one thing, a parish priest was accused of a crime by one of the English barons, who promptly hunted the priest down and killed him. That action was against the law, as only the Church had the right to discipline priests and nuns in those days. Thomas appeared before Henry II, demanding that the baron be punished for his crime. King Henry, of course, almost fell off his throne when he heard Thomas's demand. His old friend Thomas à Becket was gone, and now he faced the Archbishop of Canterbury, a formidable, stern enemy who was not awed by royal titles.

In order to get rid of Thomas and his defense of the Church, Henry II plotted with other foes of the Archbishop and managed to exile him in shame. It did not matter that the accusations made were false. Thomas Becket was thrown out of England. He went immediately to Rome, but the English bishops had already visited the pope, Alexander III, and had filled his ears with their side of the dispute.

When asked about the various charges against him, Thomas Becket admitted that he had not been given the See of Canterbury in a proper way, and he also admitted that he was not qualified for the position. Taking off his ring and his cross, he tried to give them to the pope, who refused them. The Holy Father told him not to abandon Canterbury because that would mean abandoning the honor of the Church. He did advise, however, that it would be wise for Thomas to enter a monastery for a time.

Thomas and a companion happily did just that. They stayed in a French monastic house for some time, content to be there. The See (or Archdiocese) of Canterbury remained empty, because the pope would not allow Henry II to replace Thomas Becket without an investigation and a decision from Rome.

Finally, on December 1, 1170, Becket returned to England. He had made a friend in France, King Louis VII, who believed in the conversion of Thomas Becket and wanted to see him reconciled with his own monarch. The French king also knew that he would face political problems if Thomas remained in France as a guest. Louis made peace between Henry II and his former friend, and Thomas took up his work once again as the defender of the faith in the isles.

The peace was short-lived, naturally, because the king felt betrayed by Thomas's careful watch over events. By the end of 1170, in fact, Henry II once again was ranting and raving around his castle, because his plots were being stopped at every turn by Thomas, whose sharp mind was capable of seeing through them. No matter what Henry tried, Thomas countered with some brilliant defense. In desperation one night, Henry II, seated with some of his mindless knights, asked: "Who will rid me of this turbulent priest?"

On December 29, 1170, Thomas Becket entered the cathedral of Canterbury with his trusted companion and started preparations for the Mass. Four knights of Henry II appeared in the sanctuary with swords drawn and with murder on their minds. The Archbishop told them that they were violating the cathedral and ordered them to put away their swords. The knights only laughed. They had come to take care of Henry II's problems, and they had no intention of allowing the Archbishop of Canterbury to leave the altar alive.

Thomas Becket, dying of wounds inflicted by the knights, sighed and asked for the prayers of Saint Denis and Saint Alphege of Canterbury, two martyred bishops. Praying and giving his soul to God, Thomas Becket fell silent at the altar of the Cathedral. The Archbishop's companion, a young monk, perished trying to defend him.

When word of the murders raced across England, Henry II was horrified. His rash words, his unreasonable hatred, and his ambitions had put him into a terrible political position. The pope and other Christian leaders in the world were even more horrified. Henry II and his knights were excommunicated, and the king had to make a public penance in order to restore peace and his own standing in the Church and in the country.

In the meantime, a shrine had been erected to Thomas at Canterbury. Many stories were being told throughout the land about miracles happening there, especially among the poor, whom Thomas Becket had cared for while he was Archbishop.

The four knights who had murdered Thomas suffered excommunication for a time, but it is not recorded that they were punished for the murder. The blame fell clearly on the shoulders of King Henry II, and the public penance fell there as well. After putting off the ceremony as long as possible, King Henry had to appear as a penitent and sinner at the shrine of Thomas Becket in July, 1174. There, in front of the English people and the representatives of the Church, he was stripped of his shirt and lashed by stout monks. He then made his way to

Thomas's sarcophagus (a Greek word for a stone tomb), and there he suffered more.

In life Thomas had always been the brightest one, the best. In death he triumphed not only for himself but for the honor of the Church.

Thomas Becket was canonized by Pope Alexander III in 1173, and his shrine remained a site for pilgrims through the centuries. He is honored in the Church calendars on the day of his death each year, December 29.

Brendan the Voyager

Chapter 3

Brendan the Voyager

While most Americans recognize Christopher Columbus as the explorer who discovered the New World in 1492, there are others who are also honored for making the same discovery, perhaps far earlier than Columbus and his three small ships. For example, the Vikings sailed into the New World in their great dragon ships centuries before Columbus. None of these exciting voyages would have been possible if the adventurous individuals of the Dark Ages had not dared the elements and risked defying the terrible legends which showed the sea as an enemy.

In the Dark Ages, people believed the earth was flat, like a plate. They also believed that the earth rested on the back of a hideous monster that liked to eat humans. The legend said that people foolish enough to sail out into the ocean, away from dry land, crossed the horizon and fell off into the mouth of the waiting beast. Their relatives never saw them again. The picture in this chapter is from an old painting of Brendan the Voyager, which portrays the creature that sat drooling and looking forward to the crazy people who sailed off the edge and offered themselves as a nice warm lunch.

Saint Brendan the Voyager did not end up in the belly of a beast, although we don't know for certain how far he ventured out to sea either. Some people think he visited all kinds of places, but other people do not. His voyages, however, are a part of historical record and a topic of endless debate.

Events that took place in the distant past are almost always viewed in different ways by modern scholars, and the accomplishments of Brendan the Voyager are no exception. All that is known about his adventures on the waves is the fact that he did sail *somewhere*, because the historians of his time gave him the title of "Voyager." How far he went with his holy companions, and in what sort of vessel, is a matter for ongoing debate. Brendan didn't have a television camera crew with him to videotape the journeys and to offer updates on the Late Nite News! His people kept some records, of course, but they didn't know that later generations would be arguing over their adventures.

Actually, sailing across wild seas in wind and rain and gales did not leave the crews much time for taking notes. Brendan had a remarkable memory, however, and his later accounts have added to the historical arguments about his real destination.

In Brendan's day the Irish sailed in vessels called *coracles* that skimmed across the waters. The *coracles* were small and covered with animal skins. They could be swamped by the great waves of the sea and driven onto reefs or shoals by storms. Because of the dangers of any sea voyage — real or imagined — Brendan may have constructed a stouter ship, or perhaps may have led a small navy. From records which show the number of companions which accompanied Brendan, it's evident that he either had a larger boat or several of them.

No one knows exactly why Brendan and his companions sailed where they did. Perhaps he and his companions were people who wanted to see for themselves what waited over the distant horizon — even if it *was* a monster! Most likely, knowing Brendan's life story, the men went in search of souls to be saved. A similar adventurous spirit is alive today, as we can watch in the space shuttle missions.

Brendan was born in what is the modern city of Tralee, in County Kerry, Ireland in A.D. 484. It was a dark time in the world, a period in history when great barbarian tribes were free to pillage the countryside. Pillaging is an old word for robbing one's neighbor blind. The Roman Empire no longer existed to protect them and people everywhere prayed that no crazy barbarians would come to ruin their neighborhoods.

The culture of the world — the arts, literature, music, and knowledge — was protected by the Church alone. Monks and nuns, living in small communities scattered across the wilderness, studied literature and history, and copied old masterpieces, protecting human history and knowledge. This was a time when few men and women could read or count beyond their fingers and toes. They struggled so hard to survive that their lack of education didn't bother them.

Plagues of disease swept across entire countries; fires, storms, and natural disasters cut down the populations of whole continents without mercy. Those who managed to survive the disasters were affected by the tragedies. Anyone who is forced to watch his or her neighbors die or his or her village burn to the ground at least gets a big nervous. The survivors of each new disaster began to believe in strange superstitions and started persecuting anyone they felt endangered the local community. For example, if a man's eyes were too narrow, he might be considered a menace. Or if a child was born with a twisted limb, he or she was marked as evil and quite promptly slain. These actions may have made the survivors feel that they were doing something about the tragedies — fighting back in a way, but it certainly did not do much for the innocent victims they murdered.

In the middle of such chaos and terror, the Church alone held firm to the faith, as well as to knowledge and the arts. People in the monasteries and convents tried to help those suffering outside by feeding and clothing the survivors. These monks and nuns did not adopt the superstitions going on around them. Instead, each convent and monastery tried to protect the cultural heritage of the people and to foster not only belief in God but a seeking of order, beauty, and true knowledge. One women who did this was Saint Ita, an abbess of Ireland, who served as a beacon of faith in that land.

As a lad, Brendan was recognized as having more than the usual amount of brains and abilities, and he was placed in Ita's care. She trained him and saw him ordained as a priest of the Church. The world needed brave men who could think about life, seek the truth about God, and also understand the laws of science. Brendan did not fail Saint Ita. He embarked on a rather strange career, and in so doing, became part of legend and history.

Brendan built monasteries wherever he went, and he was not the type of man to stay in one area for very long. Brendan began to explore the wilderness, on land and sea, taking a band of companions with him. Some records state that 60 individuals were with him; others give estimates ranging from 18 to 150.

The voyage that brought him historical fame lasted about seven years and was told in a book called *The Voyage or Wanderings of Saint Brendan*. He and his companions were supposedly looking for "the Land of Paradise," whatever that was. In that time, legends claimed that all sorts of creatures — such as elves — went west when they left the earth.

Some historians believe that Brendan and his companions traveled only as far as the outermost islands of Ireland, which should not have taken them seven years (unless no one on board the ship could read a map, a chart, or the stars in the night sky). Some records show Brendan and his fellow monks landing on islands off the coast of Africa — the Canaries, Madeiras, or the Azores. The most startling destination given by some historians is North America. They point to the fact that part of Chesapeake Bay on the east coast of the United States was once called "Greater Ireland." The Shawnee Indian legends also tell of a group of white men landing in their territory.

The Canary Islands were probably his ultimate goal, because his vessel or, if he had a fleet of ships, his *armada*, would not have survived the trip across the Atlantic Ocean unless he had fair winds and sunshine all the way. Sailing as far as the Canary Islands — called "the Promised Land of the Saints" — was quite a navigational feat for the era.

Brendan, however, really amazed everyone by giving accounts of the plants and animals that he discovered when landing at his final destination, *wherever* that was. Some of these plants and animals are indigenous to (can only be found on) the North American continent. Brendan's descriptions, and the fact that these plants and animals existed only in the New World, complicate the historical debates even more.

The Irish people who stayed at home when Brendan and his companions sailed away probably gave up waiting for their return after a time, believing that they had all been lost, or had ended up in the belly of the beast. After all, everyone had warned Brendan and his friends what lurked beyond the horizon. The local Irish must have mourned the loss of Brendan even as they said, "We told him so!"

Seven years is a long time, especially in those days when people did not live very long. Life on land was hard, and on the sea was even harder. Pirates sailed along the coasts and strange ships roamed over the waters, seeking victims for the slave markets of the world.

One day, however, the sail of Brendan's ship became visible on the horizon, and the people flocked to the shore to see who was landing. They were amazed when the group identified themselves, and runners raced across the land to announce their return.

Brendan and his fellow voyagers told of their discoveries and described the places, people, plants, and animals that they had seen during the years. He was not content, however, to "rest on his laurels" — that is, to sit down and talk about his accomplishments. People get tired of listening to the same tales over and over, and Brendan knew that there was work to be done in the world.

With his companions he set out again, starting monasteries throughout Ireland. He is known to have visited the Hebrides,

Scotland, Wales, and even Brittany, on the mainland of Europe. The Celtic people had settled in Ireland and all of these other places, and all spoke the same language. Even today, for example, a person coming from parts of Brittany in France can make himself or herself understood in Ireland and Scotland.

Brendan also spent three years in Britain, and he visited the famed Blessed Isle of Iona. Returning to Ireland at last, he started the beautiful Clonfert Monastery, still a glory of the land. Exhausted and advanced in age, Brendan died while visiting his sister, who was a nun in a nearby convent. Knowing that people would begin to make demands about where he was buried, he told his companions to keep his death a secret until they could get his body back to Clonfert, where he was buried without any fuss. Historians give the date of his death as 577, 578, or 583.

The rule of the spiritual life that he established at Clonfert Monastery was supposedly dictated to him by an angel, and it was maintained in the monastery for centuries. While he was a holy man, a priest dedicated to the service of God and the Church, Brendan brought something else to his vocation (his calling to the religious life). He brought a spirit of curiosity, of adventure, of wanting to know the secrets of the unexplored world. Above all, he brought faith to his voyages and explorations. It took genuine courage and belief in the providence of God to sail out into the unknown in those days. Brendan's life became an Irish epic, repeated over and over to new generations around the hearth fires.

The superstitions, legends, and ignorance about natural things scared most people during his historical period and kept them from daring to do anything. Worst of all, because of the hard times, the people of Brendan's era were afraid to think of themselves as worthwhile individuals or to dream of anything out of the ordinary.

Brendan, returning from seven years on ocean waves and far shores, represented something deep and healing for his own people. To this day, his adventurous spirit calls to people everywhere. Historians may argue over the details of his voyages, but they cannot dim the courage and the daring of Brendan and his companions. His feast day is May 16th.

Mother Frances Cabrini

Chapter 4

Mother Frances Cabrini

Nowadays people in America are worried about the numbers of immigrants and refugees entering our country, legally and illegally. Because of hard economic times and other changes, Americans today have a different view of people coming to the United States to fulfill their dreams.

After America's fight for independence from Britain, immigrants were generally welcomed in the new country (except, of course, by the Native Americans, who were not thrilled at seeing more white people invade their homeland). There were some groups of immigrants that arrived in America and were not made to feel at home, but most citizens, immigrants themselves, seemed to realize that the country was big enough to hold everybody arriving on its shores. Americans knew that they needed every man, woman, and child they could find to spread across the large continent so that other nations would not try to claim any of the territories the young United States planned on taking for itself in time. Many European countries wanted slices of the continent, and some already had parts of territories, won in past wars and conquests and considered worth fighting for against the infant land called America.

Over the years both the good and the bad arrived on America's shores as a result of our open-door policy concerning immigrants. On March 31, 1889, the United States immigration officials welcomed a future saint into the country, although they couldn't know that. Her fellow immigrants probably did not think she was anyone special either. People are sometimes slow to admit that another person might be specially favored by Almighty God.

Her name was Frances Xavier Cabrini and she was the foundress of a religious congregation of women called the Missionary Sisters of the Sacred Heart. In time she would be called "the Mother of Immigrants," but when she first arrived in America few people could see that far ahead.

Mother Cabrini was born near Pavia in Italy in 1850, the youngest of 13 children. She was educated by her sister, Rosa, who was a highly trained teacher and took a special interest in her. Frances was always attracted to the religious (or convent) life and she hoped to become a missionary for the Church, serving in some distant land.

Her parents, however, decided that she should become a schoolteacher. During the 1800s, young daughters *did not* defy the orders of their parents. Teenagers in those days didn't believe they were the smartest people on earth. They tried to understand that their parents, who had managed to stay alive for decades, were the best guides for them concerning career and other life decisions.

Agreeing with her parents' wishes, Frances studied and passed the test to enter the teaching academy. But when she was 18 and ready to attend the school, her parents died. Their sudden deaths shocked everyone.

Left alone, and now needing to work for a living, Frances became involved in orphanage work in a place operated by the Church. Although Frances was given many duties in the orphanage, she was very intelligent, organized and handled them well. Too well, as far the foundress was concerned; Frances made her and the others look bad, which can upset people.

The foundress was annoyed, but others recognized that God had sent a leader into their midst. Frances was a decent, pious, kindly soul with brains, a combination that wins over almost everyone, except the foundress of the orphanage.

Seven other young women of the town joined Frances, and she asked the local bishop for permission to found a religious congregation dedicated to the Sacred Heart and to the work of educating other young women. Her congregation proved a success, and in time she was invited to Rome, the Eternal City, where she opened two more schools. Slowly and surely Mother Cabrini was winning allies because of her piety (or holiness) and because of her intelligence.

Then a message came from Archbishop Michael Corrigan of New York, asking Mother Cabrini to bring some of her Sisters to America to work among the immigrants there. Wondering about the invitation, Mother Cabrini went to her friend, the pope, Leo XIII, to ask his opinion. Now, most people don't run to the pope normally with their problems. The fact that Mother Cabrini could turn to him shows how much she was valued by the Holy Father and how much she used obedience to the Vatican as the source of her strength.

The pope knew that Mother Cabrini had hoped to send members of her congregation to the East (Asia) as missionaries, but he felt that this was God's will showing itself to her concerning her life's work. "Not in the East," Pope Leo XIII declared, "but in the West."

Taking his advice and accepting the invitation, Mother Cabrini set sail from Italy with six of her Sisters in 1889, despite the fact that she was terrified at the thought of traveling over water. As a small child she had fallen into a river and almost drowned, which was enough to make her hesitant about going near any water larger than a bathtub!

With genuine fear, Mother Cabrini boarded an ocean liner and set sail. With the help of God, she must have overcome this phobia because throughout the rest of her life she would sail back and forth over the Atlantic Ocean 23 times.

When she arrived in New York, Mother Cabrini discovered that the Archbishop's plans for her and the Sisters had fallen apart. Not only was there no orphanage ready for the Sisters, there wasn't even a room for them to stay in the first night. They had to accept temporary lodgings and found themselves living in a filthy hole. There were no motels with big neon signs in those days. When people were stranded, they were really stranded.

The next day Mother Cabrini received another shock. She was advised by an official of the Church in New York that it would be better for her and the Sisters to return to Italy. Just like that, "Hello and goodbye!" The official added that nothing could be accomplished as originally planned. The archdiocese had no use for the Sisters or Mother Cabrini.

Mother Frances Cabrini listened and then smiled. If the officials thought that they could drag these determined women halfway around the world for nothing, and then put them on another boat heading for home, they were sadly mistaken. Americans in general, and this official in particular, knew nothing about the marvelous, compassionate woman who had arrived in the New World.

Mother Cabrini did not argue; instead she made plans of her own. She asked questions in the local Italian community, listened to various rumors, and met with groups that knew about the situation. She quickly discovered that Archbishop Corrigan had meant well, but had quarreled with the original patroness of the orphanage. Since Mother Cabrini had dealt with a difficult foundress before, this woman held no terrors for her.

She went to see the woman and talked her into reconciling with the Archbishop so that the orphanage could become a reality. Things started humming rather quickly then, as Mother Cabrini worked on her own schedule, being quite unwilling to accept delays, excuses, alibis, or reasons for failure. She had things running so smoothly, in fact, that several months later she was able to return to Italy to bring back more Sisters. She also took two young American women to Rome to begin their novitiate (or their time of training) in the congregation.

It is difficult for Americans of today to imagine what the early immigrants to the country faced when they arrived. Neighborhood names — like "Hell's Kitchen" — show that the immigrants discovered quickly that this was not the land of milk and honey, not paved with gold. Arriving in America after terrible sea voyages, the immigrants were exhausted. They had spent too many days in the cheapest part of the ships. This means they traveled in the cavernous holds of the ship, crammed with bodies and narrow beds. When they arrived, the immigrants had to stand in long lines, pass physicals, answer many questions, wear misspelled name tags, obtain official papers, and finally enter a new world that was bewildering and alarming.

For many the beginnings were made worse by the fact that the immigration officials could not spell their original European names, which is why their name tags were misspelled. The officials would write down American names that sounded something like their original ones or sometimes just renamed whole families something simple like "Smith" or "Jones." If the immigrants wanted to stay in America they had to accept the new names.

When they had passed through the immigration center, if no one was there to meet them, they were on their own, hoping to the good God that they would find someone, somewhere, who spoke their old language. They dragged their suitcases through the streets until they saw store signs that they could read and understand, then hunted for rooms and jobs and began their upward journey, seeking the American dream.

As a result, different neighborhoods in cities like New York became ethnic centers, the destinations of the various types of immigrants arriving in the country. They banded together to preserve their peace of mind, their traditions, and their safety in a foreign land.

One neighborhood was called "Little Italy" in New York City, and Mother Cabrini targeted the area for her mission work. She started outreach programs and she searched for children and young girls who were in danger, offering them protection. Her work did not end in New York. She went to other American cities, taking Sisters with her, and started programs as far away as Nicaragua.

Mother Cabrini was slow in learning English, mainly because she was so busy. Recognizing the medical needs of others, in 1892 she founded Columbus Hospital in New York, on the 400th anniversary of the discovery of the New World by the explorer. She also traveled to Central and South America, and to France and England, becoming a familiar face in the ghettos of the entire world.

By 1907 there were more than 1,000 members of the Missionary Sisters of the Sacred Heart. Mother Cabrini had founded 50 institutions in eight countries. Even the inmates of the dreaded Sing Sing prison in New York sent her a beautifully illuminated message when she celebrated a jubilee (a 50th anniversary).

Mother Cabrini became an American citizen in 1909. Two years later she started showing signs of exhaustion, the result of her unending labors. She died alone on December 22, 1917, in one of her convents in Chicago. The entire nation mourned her passing because she had won the respect of people of all faiths. In 1946, Mother Frances Xavier Cabrini was canonized as America's first saint, the Mother of Immigrants. Her feast day is November 13th.

Father Charbel Makhlouf

Chapter 5

Father Charbel Makhlouf

Many American Catholics think that the Masses and other religious services they attend, which are all conducted according to the western tradition, or Roman (also called Latin) Rite, are the only forms of Catholic worship in the world. Because they were raised in the Roman style, people cannot imagine that other Catholics might use different types of prayers, hymns, or liturgies (that is, worship services).

That isn't a very accurate picture of the Church, because there's a reason it has historically been called "universal." The Catholic Church has never been limited to one language or one set of traditions, because Christ commanded his followers to bring the Gospel — the "Good News" — to men and women *everywhere.*

People in other countries of the world would be surprised if they knew that Roman Rite Catholics have never heard of their different liturgical styles and ceremonies. Such Catholics in other lands use words, music, architecture and even vestments (the priest's robes) that reflect their own heritage.

Because the Catholic Church is alive and well in countries all over the earth, the liturgies of these Churches (as they are called to identify the membership in each nation) are closely connected to local languages, customs, and traditions. The Churches are part of other "Rites," set apart by the Holy See to meet the needs of the various nationalities. There are many interesting and ancient Rites within the Catholic family across the world. They have been in use since the time of the Apostles, who went throughout the world preaching about the Risen Christ. While the various Rites may be unique, all are in union with Rome and accept the supremacy (or authority) of the pope.

In the country called Lebanon, located north of modern Israel on the Mediterranean Sea, Catholics worship God in the Eastern Rite styles. Lebanon was called Phoenicia in the ancient world, and its people were known as fearless sailors who traveled the waves. Lebanon is mentioned in the Bible and in other historical records as well. Countries on Lebanon's borders wanted the great cedar trees that once stood as giants throughout the land. Cedar wood was prized everywhere in the ancient world, especially by the Egyptians and then by the Romans.

Some of the Christians in Lebanon are called the Maronites (Catholics belonging to the Maronite Rite). This form of liturgy dates back to the early Christian era, to the time of the Apostles and early missionaries. Saint Maron (also called Saint Maro) lived in Lebanon at the time of Saint John Chrysostom, called "the Golden-Tongued." When Saint John came to Lebanon to tell the people about Christ and the Church, Saint Maron listened to him and converted, bringing other Lebanese into the faith with him. Today, there are Maronites in the United States and other countries, as well as in Lebanon.

Saint Maron did not try to make Romans out of his own people just because they had accepted Christ. He did not ask them to put aside their normal language, Aramaic (the language spoken in the time of Christ). Latin, the language of Rome, was not adopted by the Maronites for their services. In time, as Lebanon and other countries in the region were taken over by the Arab peoples, Arabic became the official language of the area. The liturgy of the Maronites is conducted in Aramaic and Arabic in Lebanon. In the United States it is conducted in Aramaic and English.

The Maronite Rite reflects centuries of Middle Eastern traditions, with beautiful rhythms and melodies from that part of the world. It also keeps alive the language used in Our Lord's own time, which is not heard in the western world any longer. The head of the Maronite Rite is called the Patriarch of Antioch, who not only leads the Church there but traditionally plays a role in the nation's government.

One of the best known Maronites in recent history is a monk called Charbel (or Sharbel) Makhlouf, who lived in the late 1800s in Lebanon. He was honored there by people of all faiths, especially by those who understood the beauty of a dedicated life, the goodness and value of men and women who give themselves to God.

Father Charbel was a hermit in the true sense of the word. Hermits are men and women who live away from other people. They don't move away because they are angry or sickened by what they see around them. Hermits live in isolated or lonely places, sometimes in huts, in order to be alone with God, to spend their nights and days in prayer, and to avoid wasting precious time — the "now." These are men and women who understand that the past is gone forever. They realize the future may or may not come, which leaves them with "now."

As a hermit, Father Charbel had a small house with a chapel, and he lived alone there, praying and talking to God. Now, conversations between friends can go on forever. Two people who understand one another have all kinds of things to say. School friends, for example, talk all day together and then call one another on the telephone to talk even more in the afternoons and evenings. Between friends there is no end to what can be shared and discussed, and no topic is boring.

The saints are called "the Friends of God," which means that most of them carried on conversations with God, and they never ran out of things to say. Father Charbel was one of these people. He prayed night and day, endlessly, and he gave praise to God on behalf of all the people in the world who have forgotten that God exists. When he was not praying, Father Charbel did not say anything at all — not one word.

Most people in the world never *stop* talking. No matter how silly the subject, they discuss it endlessly. Some human beings, in fact, hate silence. Talk fills up their ears and their lives, but it is only talk, not knowledge; words, not ideas; slogans, not faith. These people seem to hate silence — or perhaps they're frightened of it. Noise drowns out the small voice that tells them that they are wasting hours and days on nothing, and that God may have something better for them to do.

Silence is part of a hermit's life; penance is also. Father Charbel slept on a goatskin, rather than a bed. He ate no meat or fruit as a sacrifice, probably because he liked the taste of them, and he lived this way for 23 years. Silence, fasting, prayer, and penance were the hallmarks (the defining signs) of his life as a monk.

Now this does not mean that Father Charbel grew insensitive to what was going on around him. He just had a different way of looking at life. He also seemed to know things that others did not, having a special link to eternity.

One day a messenger came to tell Father Charbel that a good friend, another hermit, was dying in a nearby settlement. Father Charbel started out with the messenger, walking quickly on the dirt road so that he could be at his friend's side during the last moments of the man's life. Suddenly the monk stopped in the middle of the road, at about the halfway point of the journey. When his companion turned to urge him along, Father Charbel quietly stated that there was no need for him to go to see the man any longer. Much to the messenger's surprise, the hermit turned on his heel and he was left standing alone in the road.

Thinking Father Charbel was crazy, the messenger ran all the way to the other priest's bedside to tell him. He arrived to hear the priest had died. Actually, as the messenger and everyone else discovered, the priest died at the very moment that Father Charbel stopped in the middle of the road. He had known that there was no need for him to rush to the bed of a man already dead and gone. It was too late for consolations or kind words. He and his priest friend would meet only at the Throne of God, in eternity.

Death holds no terrors for men and women like Father Charbel, who understand that it is a natural part of living on the earth. Dying is only the putting aside of flesh and bones, a doorway to eternal life with God. The Friends of God learn this great truth early in their lives.

Father Charbel Makhlouf, Lebanon's beloved Maronite hermit, put aside his own prayers, penance, and silence on Christmas Eve, 1898. After his death, he amazed and thrilled his own people and others by working miracles and becoming a warm, compassionate friend to those in need. His canonization, recognized by the entire Catholic Church, brings honor not only to Father Charbel but to an entire group of devout Catholics who have maintained their own ways and traditions in the Maronite Rite through the ages. His feast day is December 24th.

Clare

Chapter 6

Clare

Saint Clare, the lovely friend of Francis of Assisi, is the patroness of modern television viewing, because Almighty God provided a very special type of miraculous display for her on her deathbed, which others with her also witnessed. Some people think that Saint Lucy should be the patroness of TV because she is usually shown holding her eyeballs in her hands. That image relates to moderns who sit up watching the late news shows or the Late, Late, Late Movie Theater on TV.

Clare was born in the city of Assisi in Italy in 1193 or 1194, in the exciting historical period that witnessed the Crusades and the great Holy Roman Empire. It was an age when men and women were thinking in new ways of seeing life and art, of increased trade between regions, and of interest in discovering new things about other cultures. The Renaissance was about to dawn upon the world.

During the time Clare was growing up in a fine house as the daughter of Ortolana di Fiumi and Faverone Offreduccio, a prosperous merchant of Assisi and his wife, she had every advantage and enjoyed the fruits of the Renaissance. She was beautiful, wealthy, and educated, and she could look forward to a bright future with a young man from a family of equal standing.

It was important to families in those days that their sons and daughters marry into equally wealthy or powerful families. They felt there was no sense wasting fortunes on something as silly and short-lived as love. Sons and daughters inherited the money and the titles of the family. For this reason one of them could not marry someone who wasn't of the same wealth and social class. People didn't marry their sweethearts. Marriages in those days were important alliances, involving entire generations of families and their lands and wealth.

As the beautiful daughter of a wealthy man, Clare knew how marriages were arranged, and that a similar union was planned for her. But she had also heard stories about the young man called Francis, who was setting Assisi on its ear with his different way of life. Everyone talked about him and had different opinions on his behavior. After all, he lived like a "bum" out in the country, rebuilt churches, sang songs to the sun and the moon, and tamed wild wolves.

Francis of Assisi was a Knight of Poverty. He had put aside his rank, his money, and his inheritance to serve Christ, which was considered odd, even if it was romantic, by the townspeople. Clare talked about Francis with her sisters, Beatrice and Agnes, and they watched as Francis and some of his new followers came into town to ask for food and funds for their church repairs.

When Clare was 18 years old, a bit beyond the time when she should have married according to the customs of the period, she heard Francis preaching the Lenten sermons at San Giorgino Church in Assisi. She went to him quietly after the talk and told him that she felt she had a religious vocation (a calling to the life of a nun). Francis encouraged her, but both of them knew that Clare's parents would not be thrilled with the idea at all.

Her parents, naturally, thought she was going through a phase when she casually mentioned the subject, and they did everything they could to talk her out of it. Becoming a nun was bad enough, they argued, but the idea of a high-ranking young woman living like the "bums" of Francis was something they didn't even want to think about. Women of high class didn't dress in rags and live in huts. If a young woman felt that God called her to the convent, there were plenty of traditional ones that allowed women to keep their rank and privileges.

Clare listened and went on with her life and normal routines, knowing that her parents could become very upset if pushed the wrong way. She had a secret ally, however, one that even she didn't know about.

The bishop of Assisi was a smart man, and he kept an eye on everybody and everything in town, so he did not miss what was happening to Clare Offreduccio. On Palm Sunday, 1212, everyone was in the Assisi cathedral for the blessing of the palms, a service conducted by the bishop. People liked to go to Church, and they dressed up in their best and took the front row seats so their friends and neighbors would see how good and saintly they were.

When the palms were being handed out during the service, people pushed toward the front and reached over the heads of their neighbors for them. Clare, however, was suddenly filled with anxiety and stayed in her pew, perhaps wondering why everyone else was acting so strangely. She couldn't push and shove her way up the aisle just to get a palm as a sign of victory over her neighbors, so she stayed in her place and prayed instead. To her astonishment, and probably to the surprise of everyone else in the church as well, the bishop walked down the aisle and handed her a palm personally. He knew that she was a special soul, called by God and chosen for a particular reason. As she apparently had not asked for his opinion officially, the bishop used the occasion to express his approval of her plans by giving her the palm in front of the entire population of Assisi.

Clare's parents may have been surprised by the scene, but they didn't take the bishop's actions seriously or as a personal statement on his part. At least they didn't keep close watch on Clare, who slipped out of the house that night and went to see Francis and his monks.

In a small chapel she put aside her beautiful robes and put on a simple coarse tunic (a gown made of rough fibers) while Francis cut off her lovely long blond hair. She put a woven cord around the waist of the loose, full-length tunic. Her head was covered with a wimple, a piece of material designed to hide her hair and to frame her face. This was covered with a black veil, the traditional nun's symbol.

Because Clare could not live with a group of monks out in the country, she went to the Benedictine convent nearby. These good nuns accepted her and started training her in the religious life, knowing that she did not intend to become one of their order but to start a group of religious women according to the Franciscan way of life.

When her parents discovered that Clare was gone, they set up a cry and started hunting for her. In time, of course, they discovered that she had gone to Francis of Assisi and had become one of his group. The family set out for the Benedictine convent to reclaim their precious daughter, but Clare had been moved to another Benedictine house by the wise old superior who knew the ways of angry parents. Then, to make matters worse for the family, Agnes, one of Clare's sisters, became a Franciscan nun too, and she received the habit from Francis and joined Clare in training.

When the uproar faded, as they always do in time, Clare and Agnes, having completed their days with the Benedictines, set up a convent next to the shrine of San Damiano, the church that Francis and his monks were rebuilding. Clare's mother (widowed by that time) and some other socially high-ranked women came to join Clare.

The order called "the Poor Clares," or the Franciscan Minoresses, was born. Within a few years it had spread throughout Italy and Europe. In Prague, in modern Czechoslovakia, for example, Princess Agnes, the daughter of the King of Bohemia, received the Franciscan habit and founded yet another convent of Poor Clares.

The women were very serious about living as Brides of Christ and about the subject of poverty. They wore coarse, roughly spun habits, but no shoes or stockings. Even in the dead of winter the Poor Clares normally go without foot coverings.

They also slept on the ground on simple pallets (beds made out of thin mattresses) and did not eat meat or anything else that tasted good at meals. The Poor Clares, who at first were called the "Poor Ladies of San Damian," simply "ate to live."

The harshness of the rule of life used by the Poor Clares alarmed many people outside the convent, of course. These were people who preferred to see others stay "in the middle of the road," for life to stay balanced. Women like Clare, who upset the traditional order of life, made other people feel uncomfortable and look bad.

The Poor Clares and the followers of Francis changed the age in which they lived by upsetting the "balance" that some wanted in place in the Church and in the world. But life wasn't really "balanced" at all. People in the upper classes had rich clothes, big houses, and plenty of food. They didn't care that people in the lower classes didn't have warm clothes, dry houses, and enough to eat.

By living in true poverty the Poor Clares reminded everyone that each human being is born to fulfill all that God asks of them, and to die when that has been accomplished. Money, titles, even popularity can't add a single moment to a person's life.

The Poor Clares were living testimony of this truth about human existence. Pope Gregory IX had agreed to their rule of life, "a privilege to poverty," because Clare insisted upon it. This meant that she and her sisters didn't have to be shielded from suffering, or be considered weak and fragile. They could embrace the hard life of poverty and the commands of Christ with the same enthusiasm and staying power that the men brought to their Franciscan monasteries. Clare — throughout her long years of service — believed that, and her fellow nuns proved she was right.

Clare and the other nuns were part of the Franciscan family, but their rule, which kept them in a cloister (an enclosed convent) did not allow any of them to leave or to take part in outdoor activities. Clare was appointed the head of her community in 1215 and served for many years. By 1253, however, it became obvious that Clare was about to make her way to heaven. Pope Innocent IV, the Holy Father at the time, visited her in her cell (her room in the convent) twice before she died.

During her final hours, Mass was being celebrated in the chapel of the Poor Clare convent, but Clare was too close to death to be moved to the altar. Before her astonished eyes, the wall in her room melted away, and Clare, still in her bed, could suddenly see the Mass and take part in the beloved service. Because of this she is called the patroness of television.

When she died just a short time later, all of Italy wept. The pope canonized Clare two years after her death, as her order spread throughout the world. The Poor Clares have not diminished over the years but have remained true to Clare's vision. Many dioceses have convents of Poor Clares, who carry on this beautiful way of life. Saint Clare's feast day is August 11th.

Damien de Veuster

Chapter 7

Damien de Veuster

On May 10, 1873, a young priest of the Sacred Hearts Congregation stepped off a steamer and onto the pier of a place called Kalaupapa, on the Hawaiian island of Molokai. Kalaupapa is located on a peninsula — a rocky, barren area that juts out into the sea and is cut off from the main portions of Molokai Island by steep cliffs. The young priest's name was Damien de Veuster, and by taking those steps he changed the lives of hundreds of thousands of people who suffered the terrible disease known throughout history as leprosy, now called Hansen's Disease.

Leprosy has been known since ancient times, even before Christ. It's a disease that attacks the skin and nerves, and causes the skin to swell and become lumpy and discolored. Although leprosy isn't a disease people always die from, it weakens them and makes it easier for them to die of something else. Now people in every age of the world were terrified by even the name of the disease. As a result, the victims of leprosy were treated to really horrible acts of cruelty by their families and friends.

People were so afraid of catching leprosy that they would even pretend their loved ones were dead. Persons with leprosy were covered over with black veils and made to stand in freshly dug graves. The priest then recited the services of burial for them — even though they were still very much alive — and relatives called goodbye from a safe distance. When the service was over, the ill persons were told to leave town and never come back. It was just as if they had died.

Kicked out of their homes, people with leprosy had to roam the back roads, hiding in caves and hoping that the next town wouldn't set their dogs on them. Even small children discovered to have leprosy were treated with the same horror and contempt. Unfortunately, people who developed minor skin rashes were often labeled as "lepers" by mistake and were treated to the same cruelty. Sometimes, people believed that having leprosy was a punishment for sins. The horrible lumps on their bodies supposedly represented the sins of their souls.

Today the medical world knows that leprosy is caused by a rod-shaped bacteria called *Mycobacterium leprae (M. leprae)*. Dr. Gerhard Hansen discovered the bacteria not too long after Damien landed on Molokai. Of course, these scientific breakthroughs by Dr. Hansen and others were not known in Hawaii when the young priest started his work among the patients on the island. He might as well have been back in the Middle Ages because the leprosy victims of his time were shown the same cruelty. The infected persons were captured, thrown on ships, and taken to Molokai, where it was hoped they would die quietly under the tropical sun, out of sight and out of mind.

Damien, landing among them, changed that outlook for all time, because he gave leprosy a human dimension. He treated each leprosy victim as what he or she was — a human being in need. He had arrived to care for a group of leprosy victims who had been exiled from the other Hawaiian Islands, but his arrival signalled a new understanding and a new period of medical care for the stricken.

Damien was born in Tremeloo, Belgium, on January 3, 1840. He was called Joseph by his family, and had followed his brother, Pamphile, into the Sacred Hearts community. Damien was not a likely candidate for the religious life in the eyes of many people. He was heavy-set, healthy, muscular, and seemed a little slow. This slowness was not stupidity, but rather a natural sense of quiet and a reluctance to speak up in the presence of people he believed were smarter than he was. Even today some people do not expect the big, muscular people of the world to be particularly bright.

Actually, Damien was at first considered too dumb to learn even basic Latin, so he was not viewed by his fellow monks as a potential priest. Pamphile, who was a scholarly person, believed in Damien's ability and took the time to teach him Latin, and as a result, the young man was accepted for holy orders (ordination to the priesthood).

Before being made a priest, however, Damien volunteered for the mission in the Hawaiian Islands, where the Sacred Hearts fathers and sisters had been working for decades. Originally, Pamphile had been chosen, but he had fallen seriously ill. Accepted in Pamphile's place by the superiors of the Sacred Hearts fathers, Damien set sail with others and became part of the Hawaiian missionary team.

Damien was ordained in the Cathedral of Our Lady of Peace in Honolulu in 1864 and sent to the Big Island of Hawaii. The Big Island is a marvelous tourist destination today because it is so huge, and because volcanos roar and send streams of flaming lava into the night sky. In Damien's time there were no fancy hotels or tour guides. He arrived to discover that he had been assigned to a mission composed of 2,000 square miles, marked by cliffs, deep ravines, and hidden valleys, not to mention the volcanos, one of which blew its top on several occasions during his lifetime!

In a letter to his family at home, Damien wrote: "There is nothing like it in the world to give one an idea of Hell." He didn't mention that he had to drag himself up and down ravines in order to find his parishioners. Sometimes he used a horse and other times a mule, proving himself more stubborn than the animal in a crisis.

Days blended into months, and Damien discovered the wonderful spirit of "Aloha" that was woven into the island lifestyle. The word "Aloha" means hello or goodbye, and it also stands for a gentle spirit of understanding, generosity, and kindness, a spirit still alive and active in Hawaii today. Damien faced danger and trouble in his parish, but he was also welcomed at the homes of his people, who lived the Aloha spirit wherever they were.

All of them talked about what was taking place in Hawaii, and one special problem kept coming back to haunt them. Leprosy was widespread among the Hawaiians, probably having been brought to the islands by people of other lands who migrated there to work in the various plantations. As the disease spread, the people, especially the white people who had immigrated to the islands, grew more hysterical, demanding that the government take steps to protect them.

King Kamehameha V, the ruler of Hawaii at the time, issued an order that those discovered with the disease should be exiled from their families and friends and taken to Molokai's peninsula area. For this reason, the Hawaiians began calling leprosy the "Separating Sickness." Most native islanders had no fear of the disease, and if a loved one was suffering from it they went to a great deal of trouble to hide such a family member from the police. The round-up of leprosy victims continued, however, and Molokai's peninsula began to receive boatloads of victims.

In May, 1873, Bishop Louis Maigret, SS.CC. (the initials of the Sacred Hearts), the missionary in charge of the Catholic programs in the islands at the time, held a meeting among the priests and asked for volunteers for the Molokai duty. He had to explain the dangers involved, as well as the inconveniences. Life in the colony would be one of isolation and loneliness. Even the simple food sent by the government was brought by steamer, then dumped into the water near the shore, where the crates and bundles floated to the shoreline.

Damien insisted at the meeting that he be allowed to go as a volunteer chaplain, and Bishop Maigret agreed, thinking it was only a temporary assignment. He knew that the young priest was stubborn, and he liked the enthusiasm that Damien showed for the assignment.

Perhaps without realizing it, however, the bishop was aware that the Hand of God was at work. When he accompanied the young priest to Molokai, the bishop announced that Damien would become something far more than temporary chaplain. He said: ". . . I have brought you one who will be a father to you, and who loves you so much that for your welfare and for the sake of your immortal souls he does not hesitate to become one of you, to live and die with you."

Damien, who was then only 33 years old, entered the leper colony, where the Hawaiians had put up a sign that read: *Aole Kanawai me Keia wahi*, meaning, "Here we have no law whatsoever."

Kalaupapa was a place of despair and misery as the leprosy victims tried to fight the disease and their isolation, despite the efforts of some good people to ease the situation with a clinic and care. The few courageous souls who tried to help found little support from the government and the local community and even less financial backing. They could only wait and hope, little realizing that the young priest who had just landed among them would be the solution because God had chosen him for this special role.

Horrified by what he saw, using a pipe to surround his body with the aroma of tobacco so that the smell of rotting bodies did not make him gag, Damien began to establish order. He started by gathering the young boys and girls who had been abandoned on the island. These young folks were being hurt by the older members of the settlement, who were so exhausted and in so much pain that they no longer cared about how vulnerable little children can be when abandoned by those they loved.

Damien went from hut to hut, from shelter to shelter, burying the bodies of men and women who had died alone in the bushes where they could be eaten by wild pigs and insects.

Damien's pipe billowed out great stacks of smoke when he did this work of mercy.

He soon became the nurse and surgeon of Molokai, pushing aside the despair of the patients and the indifference of others. Putting what little medicine and few bandages that he had on wounds, and even amputating limbs that were infected beyond saving, Damien used patience and charity to care for the men, women, and children of the settlement. He did have soap, water, clean linens, and some sedatives, but there were few other supplies available. Originally the leprosy victims were each given one robe and one set of linens per year — as if these would last beyond a few days.

Father Damien built 2,000 rough wooden coffins with his own hands, burying the dead himself or with the help of the stronger patients. The cemetery that he established was his nightly place of comfort. He called it his "garden of the dead," and he had placed each of the coffins into the ground himself, knowing each name and soul, and rejoicing because their suffering was over.

Damien built an orphanage for the smallest victims, and a clinic. To boost the morale of the settlement, and to give the patients something to look forward to, he held festivals, some featuring horse races. The patients could ride on horseback in the early stages of the illness, and loved to race along the shore. In those moments they were whole again, free under the sun, and alive in the beauty of the island and the sea.

By 1877, after years of work, the Hawaii Board of Health and other groups recognized the role that Damien played on Molokai. Help was on its way at last. The original plans of replacing Damien with another priest had long been forgotten, although some priests did arrive to work with him for limited periods. Also on hand was a remarkable American called Joseph Dutton, a veteran of the Civil War, who arrived and announced that Damien needed help and "good old Yankee know-how."

It was Brother Joseph, as he was called, who sent out the first word of leprosy symptoms on Damien's body. At first the priest noted small dry spots on his skin. His feet sometimes felt hot and feverish. He had nerve problems, then a lack of feeling in his left foot. It is reported that when Damien accidentally spilled boiling water on that foot he discovered he felt no pain at all.

Living with victims of leprosy, familiar with its symptoms, Damien knew what was happening, but he didn't allow the knowledge or the illness to keep him from his work. Later, when Damien was in the last stages of his illness, scarred and crippled by leprosy, visitors to the settlement found him sitting on the roof of the church, making repairs. He never stopped working because the need was there and because others depended upon him.

When he wrote to Pamphile (who had developed consumption, a lung disease), he admitted: "As for myself, I cannot hide from you for long that I am threatened by yet a more terrible disease. Leprosy, you know, is contagious. In reality I am still as robust as I always was, but for three years my left foot has lost all feeling. I have in my body a poison that threatens to spread throughout. Let's not go shouting this out, and let's pray for one another."

People nowadays announce the fact that they have the flu or a bad cold with more hysterics! Damien was telling his brother that he had received a death sentence, and his dying was not going to be easy or pleasant. He was matter of fact about it, certainly, because he had buried so many others and did not expect to be saved miraculously from their fate, which he shared willingly for the love of God.

In September, 1881, Princess Liliuokalani, the acting Queen of Hawaii, visited the settlement on Molokai, planning to give a public address there. She was so upset by the suffering that she wept instead of giving the speech. Liliuokalani was known for her gentleness, kindness, and dignity, even when facing political enemies or other problems.

On her return to Honolulu, the Queen gave Father Damien the Order of Knight Commander of the Royal Order of Kalakaua. His greatest gift, however, was the arrival of the Franciscan Sisters of Syracuse, under the leadership of their former Mother General, Marianne Kope. These Sisters started work in the islands and continued it over the decades, and are still very much a part of the Catholic programs there.

By 1885, leprosy was confirmed in Father Damien's body, and it spread rapidly through his system. He announced his condition publicly in the Chapel of Saint Philomena on Molokai, beginning his sermon not by his usual "My dear brethren" but using the shocking words: "We lepers. . ."

The press carried the story in newspapers all across the world, and letters began to pour into Molokai to express the grief of thousands of people, including royalty. Men and women everywhere began taking a close look at Father Damien and his work, calling him "The Hero of Molokai," and a closer look, too, at the cruel and ineffective treatment of leprosy victims over the centuries.

One might imagine that Damien was a patient, kindly, gentle man. Sometimes he was. Damien was the soul of patience when he cared for the people of his parish on the isle of Hawaii or for the victims of leprosy, but he was a terror to anyone who tried to ignore the needs of the people or to demand unreasonable government control of the colony. He was also practical. For example, he is reported to have saved himself time and energy by using large crackers, called saloon style, when he prepared his meals. He made a stew and piled the blend of meat and vegetables on the saloon crackers so that he could eat the food without having to use plates and wash them afterward!

When clothes and medical supplies didn't arrive on Molokai, Damien went to Honolulu, horrifying the people on board the steamer ships that carried him between the islands. Eventually, because of his disease, the captains of these steamers refused to allow him to set foot on their decks. But while he could still travel, Damien pushed carts through the streets of Honolulu, begging for necessary supplies. The hysterical reactions of people did not upset him. He had only one thing in mind, the good of his patients, and he didn't worry about frightening people if he could make good things happen for the leprosy victims on Molokai. Supplies usually came quickly as a result of his startling appearance on the streets of the Honolulu.

Damien continued his work until April 15, 1889, when, as observers noted, he died "like a child, with a smile on his face." He could rest easily because his work had taken root and was in the capable hands of others. At the time, Dr. Hansen's research was continuing, and medical researchers were developing medicines that controlled or cured the condition, now renamed Hansen's Disease in honor of Dr. Hansen.

The really shocking part of the medical breakthroughs, however, is that people in Africa, Asia, and other isolated places don't have medicine easily available to them, even today. The World Health Organization estimates that there are over 11 million leprosy victims in the world right now. Others believe that the number is even larger, especially in China and in India. One group in India, calling themselves the "Damiens," cares for more than 200,000 victims of Hansen's Disease in a single small region there. Many of these patients and their kind benefactors don't have the new medicines that could halt the progress of leprosy. Even small children, facing years of pain, aren't receiving the medicines that could help them.

For this reason Father Damien remains important today. Great leaders of all faiths wrote to the Holy Father recently to ask that Damien be given the "honors of the altar," which means the rank of Blessed or Saint. One person who signed that request was Mother Teresa of Calcutta, who operates leper colonies in several regions of the world, along with her other charitable programs. Damien may have been put to rest, but his spirit remains everywhere.

He was originally buried beside the church in Molokai, near the pandanus tree that had served as his shelter in his first days on the island. In 1936, however, Father Damien's body was removed from his island grave. The Belgian government requested that his remains be returned to his homeland, where his own people could give him honors. King Leopold III of Belgium met the casket and led his people in prayers as the Hero of Molokai was returned to his native country.

Dorothy

Chapter 8

Dorothy

There is a strange legend about Emperor Nero, who not only fiddled while Rome burned but managed to have the fires that he personally started blamed on the early Christians in the city. Nero was well known for holding so-called "games" in the arenas of Rome to distract the Romans from the fact that he was really crazy. During these games Nero murdered Christians by feeding them to lions and tigers, hanging them on crosses, setting them on fire, and subjecting them to other tortures. The Romans, with all their dignity and artistic achievements, actually brought picnics to the gory shows and ate their lunches while watching humans die in agony on the sands below them. The Colosseum in Rome still stands as a monument to these "games" and martyrs.

After busy days, during which he watched hundreds of Christian martyrs — including men, women, and children — die in the arena, Nero would walk among the corpses left on the sand as he studied their faces. The fact that most of these early martyrs died smiling drove Nero over the edge. As he walked from body to body, staring down at the smiles, his soldiers and companions watched in disgust. Driven mad by the sight of joyous faces, Nero ranted and raved and tried to think up new ways to hurt the Christians so they would lose their smiles in death.

Mad Emperor Nero would have especially hated Saint Dorothy, a Christian martyr who died laughing out loud. She was caught in the persecutions held during the reign of Emperor Diocletian, who came to the throne of Rome long after Nero was murdered in an uprising among the people. A man named Fabricius is believed to have caused Dorothy's arrest for an unknown reason. Her judge was the Roman administrator of the area of Cappadocia (a border region of modern Turkey), an official named Sapricius.

Dorothy apparently spent days in prison before her trial and execution, and during this time she managed to win over two women guards by her gentle Christian faith. On February 6, in the year 311, she was dragged into the court and accused of being a Christian, which was considered criminal at the time. She didn't deny the fact, admitting happily to one and all that she was willing to die for Christ.

This brought about an unusual response from another Roman, a lawyer named Theodosius. He called out, "Bride of Christ, send me some fruits from your bridegroom's garden!" Everyone laughed, and Theodosius went home, thinking he had won friends by insulting this young woman. Soon after, however, there was a knock at his door, and a small boy (some versions of the story claim it was an angel) stood on his doorstep, holding a headdress wrapped in a simple cloth. Theodosius recognized the headdress as Dorothy's. He also saw three roses and three apples in the package. Much to his surprise, he realized that Dorothy had followed his instructions — the ones that he shouted at her in hatred — and had provided him with the fruits of Christ's garden. Theodosius became a Christian and soon followed Dorothy in martyrdom.

For her execution, she was placed on a heated rack, stretched and burned as her tormentors called out insults, but she laughed as she died, knowing that Theodosius had learned the truth of the faith and knowing that the two women wardens in the prison would become Christians and spread Christ's teachings throughout the region. Dorothy's feast day is February 6th, and on that day some places have a special celebration during which trees are blessed.

Edmund Campion

Chapter 9

Edmund Campion

Modern Catholics and people of other faiths take their right to worship God for granted, guaranteed by law. In recent times, Communist governments in eastern Europe put people into prison for daring to stand up for the Christian faith, but governments like these have collapsed from the weight of their own corruption and economic problems. Today, few dictators dare to interfere with this basic privilege. People refuse to allow anything to get in the way of their relationship with their Creator and they can prove dangerous to tyrants who try to stop them from saying prayers in their own way.

Although freedom to worship God is a constitutional right in America and in other countries today, in the past it was not always possible to openly practice a particular faith without being in danger, even to the point of facing death. The great nation of England, the birthplace of the Magna Carta (the document proclaiming human rights and values) was once the scene of terrible religious persecutions. Both Catholics and Protestants suffered during the reigns of Henry VIII, King Edward VI, Queen Mary I, and Queen Elizabeth I.

Queen Mary I, a Catholic, took the throne after the death of young King Edward, who was the son of Henry VIII and Mary's half-brother. Queen Mary tried to bring England back into the Catholic Church by arresting and executing Protestants, and is called "Bloody Mary" by historians because of it. But Queen Elizabeth I, who had many, many Catholics tortured and slain, is always called "Good Queen Bess" by the same historians.

During the reign of Queen Elizabeth a young man began to make a name for himself as a scholar and orator. He was Edmund Campion, born in 1540, the son of a London bookseller. Lord Cecil, Elizabeth I's right-hand man, called Edmund Campion "one of the diamonds of England." This "diamond," however, soon became famous for another reason, and he was marked an enemy of the throne of England. Royal police and local constables hunted him down as a result, and eventually he was dragged to what was called "the Tree of Terrible and Bloody Memory."

The young Edmund Campion, as he gained a reputation as a speaker at Oxford University, had a bright future before him, both in the Anglican Church and in the court of Elizabeth I. He was chosen as one of the students who addressed Queen Elizabeth and Lord Cecil when they visited the school in 1566. Campion had also written a book, *History of Ireland*, which he presented to the Queen as well. She found the book remarkable and praised Edmund to her friends and courtiers.

With this entry into English political circles, Edmund became the toast of London and was praised when he began studying for the priesthood in the newly established Anglican Church. Many predicted that he would rise like a new star in the heavens, and he already had patrons, people willing to speak for him and to provide him with the necessary funds for his studies and writing.

Edmund Campion, however, was a true scholar, and the more he learned about the Anglican Church the graver the doubts that came into his mind and heart. He took orders in the Anglican community and received degrees and credentials (papers stating that he was all that he said he was), but then he realized that he could not continue his life as a Christian outside the Roman Catholic Church. Historically, and logically, he realized the Anglican Church was not a church at all, but a product of King Henry VIII, based on lies.

Henry VIII, who had wanted to marry another woman, asked the pope in Rome to grant him a divorce from Queen Catherine, his legal wife and consort (companion on the throne). When the pope refused, Henry declared himself the head of the Church in England and promptly gave himself permission to do what he wanted. Others agreed with him, and those who did not accept the new church and Henry's new role were put to death, saints such as Thomas More.

Realizing the historical truths concerning the Anglican Church, Edmund Campion knew that he couldn't continue to pretend to agree with something he knew in his heart was wrong. Fleeing to Douai, the English religious center in France, Edmund asked to be received into the Catholic Church and to study for the priesthood. He also joined the Jesuits in Rome in 1573, becoming part of a secret operation designed to comfort the Catholics of England and to turn the people of that country once more to the road to the faith. Lord Cecil and Queen Elizabeth hated all Catholic priests and the two particularly feared the Jesuits. They believed, therefore, that Edmund, "one of the diamonds of England," had become the enemy.

Historically, remember that Queen Elizabeth I faced enemies at home and abroad. Mary, Queen of Scots, living in nearby Scotland, announced her legitimate claim to the English throne, and there were many plots against "Good Queen Bess," started by Catholics and others. Cecil and the lords of the court felt that they were protecting the rightful monarch when they set out to track down the priests, especially Jesuits, who entered the country secretly, believing that all of them were determined to murder Elizabeth.

Campion had been marked as an enemy the moment he became a Catholic priest and a member of the Jesuit Order. That Edmund and the others were sincere in trying to comfort the English Catholics and to restore the land to the Catholic Church did not matter. In the eyes of Cecil, they were men with criminal intent, to be hunted and slain.

Edmund worked for a time in the city of Prague, Czechoslovakia, then was asked if he would volunteer to return to his homeland. The priests sent back to England knew the risks involved before they started out. The men understood that they could die at the hands of the Queen's men if they were caught.

Edmund accepted the risk, and he was sent back to England with another Catholic priest, Father Robert Persons, in 1580. Their instructions were to contact the Catholics of England, care for them and provide them with the sacraments.

Campion went into the countryside to begin his missionary work there. He wrote *Decem Rationes*, "The Ten Reasons," challenging the Anglican clergy to open debates about the validity of their faith.

The English people were still uneasy about the new Anglican faith and upset that Henry VIII had destroyed the beautiful abbeys and shrines of their land. Because of "The Ten Reasons," Edmund Campion was pursued ruthlessly. He led a dangerous and adventurous life as a result, using what were called "priests' holes" — niches or secret compartments designed to hide Catholic priests from the police. The holes were behind fireplaces, in attics, basements, or other places of Catholic homes. The police came regularly, and they had spies among the Catholics, men and women who hoped to save themselves from prison or death by turning in the priests who were sent from France to care for them.

On Sunday, July 16, 1581, Edmund Campion preached to a group of Catholics in a home in Norfolk. There was a traitor in the crowd, who turned them in, and the police came to the house, searching it from top to bottom three times. Edmund and two other priests were hidden in a small space over the gateway of the estate, and they were found there at the end of the day, as the police had information that they were on the estate and did not give up their search until they had found the men.

The priests were taken to the Tower of London, where they were tortured, then led to the "Tree of Terrible and Bloody

Memory," which was located at Tyburn. There Edmund
Campion and his companions were hung, drawn, and quartered,
a favorite and horrible method of execution, and a spectacle that
drew great crowds to watch.

Saint Henry Morse and others were among the martyrs
with Campion, all of whom were canonized in 1970. During
many of these executions, the ambassadors from the Catholic
countries of France, Spain, and Portugal risked the anger of
Queen Elizabeth I by attending the tortures. They came out of
reverence and to give the martyrs honor. It should be noted that
"one of the diamonds of England" was not forgotten by Oxford
University. Campion Hall stands in that institution today as a
tribute to his memory, his scholarship, and his courage. Saint
Edmund and the other Holy Martyrs of England are
remembered on October 25th each year.

Francis of Assisi

Chapter 10

Francis of Assisi

One of the most popular saints in the whole world, who is honored by people of all faiths, Francis of Assisi is called the *Poverello*, or the "Little Poor Man." Born in Assisi, Italy, in 1181 or 1182, Francis gave up his inheritance and social position when he was 20 or 21 and embraced the lifestyle that he believed Christ commanded of his followers. Most people know that Francis repaired Saint Damiano and the Portiuncula — a Benedictine shrine given to Francis and his followers. Most know about the great Franciscan Order, and that Francis received the stigmata (the wounds of Christ). The "Little Poor Man" remains a bright memory for men and women everywhere because he explodes like a beautiful star in the horizon of history.

Something not well known or understood is Francis' closeness to nature and all living creatures. As he is honored for his embrace of poverty, for his refusal to accept the world's terms in living out his spiritual life, so should he be honored for understanding God's creatures and the natural wonders of creation.

This is particularly important for people today, who may live in cement buildings, walk on sidewalks, and never hear a bird singing or a cricket chirping on the hearth (an old word for fireplace). Few people in this day and age have a chance to take a walk in the country each evening, and fewer understand how animals and other wild creatures live and serve God.

Francis knew that the wild creatures of the earth and nature itself shared a great secret, one that had been given to him in prayer. All living beings give praise to God by being perfect. A tree is perfect when it does all that it was created to do, and as a created perfect thing, it gives praise to God. People should be aware that they are called to the same high standards in their own lifetimes. Wise men and women honor nature, because they know that humans are part of nature, and that all were created by God.

Francis of Assisi is known for his way with wild creatures, and this is part of his lasting charm. In the region of Gubbio, Italy, for example, he heard the local people were hunting a wild wolf. The villagers claimed that the wolf was eating their flocks and soon would start eating their children. Francis, after listening to their complaints, walked out into the nearby woods and called the wolf to his side. The beautiful animal came willingly, sitting and listening to what Francis had to say.

The animal then accompanied Francis back to the village, where the locals screamed and prepared themselves for an attack. The wolf stayed beside Francis, who asked the villagers to start sharing their food with the creatures of the wild, which were starving because of the cold and bad weather. The people argued for a while but finally agreed, and one man put out his shaking hand to pet the wolf. The wolf of Gubbio was never hunted again, and the animal protected the village, which began to boast about the wild creature and Francis' visit.

Wild birds would perch in nearby trees when Francis spoke, and once, when they started twittering during a sermon, he asked them to please remain silent until he was finished. The birds stopped their noise immediately, much to the surprise of the people gathered about.

Half-frozen bees crawled to his side during the winter, seeking warmth and food, and he cared for them. Nightingales came to sing him lullabies. Even birds flew to Francis for protection against hunters.

All of this sounds strange to city people, but it does make us stop to wonder and think about past times, when men and women understood the earth and its creatures. Francis was a human being who understood that men and women are part of a circle of existence on the earth, the pattern of creation established by God.

The next time our beautiful planet earth is shown on TV from the space shuttle, notice how fragile this blue ball appears against the darkness of space. Think about Francis, who understood that all created beings on our blue ball were made by God for perfection and for giving praise. His feast day is October 4th.

Genevieve of Paris

Chapter 11

Genevieve of Paris

The beautiful city of Paris, France, remains one of the world's most delightful places. The great cathedrals, the Seine River that wends its way through the city, the feeling of joy and romance that dances through Paris streets make it a great place to visit, and thousands of people come from all over the world to spend time in the City of Lights — Paris.

Many famous people have walked the streets of Paris, and one of them, Genevieve, has earned a lasting place of reverence among the French people. Genevieve was not raised in Paris, but in a small town, Nanterre, about four miles away. She was born around A.D. 422, and was probably called Genovefa, because people talked that way in those days.

When she was seven years old, a bishop came to Nanterre, preaching and trying to build the faith in the region. He noticed Genevieve, even though she was tiny, and after one sermon spoke to her parents about her. Genevieve, he said, would become a great saint, and her parents had to take care of her, because God had entrusted them with a very special soul. When her parents recovered from their shock, they agreed.

The bishop asked Genevieve if she wanted to be a nun, and she replied she had always wanted to belong to God alone. The bishop took her into the church, and in front of the entire town he consecrated the young girl to Christ. What the villagers thought about this is not known, but they didn't interfere, and Genevieve grew up in prayer and in the ways of the "Friends of God."

When she was 15, she received the official veil (habit of a nun) from the bishop of Paris. Already the young woman was noted for her holiness, although some people laughed at her, asking her why she was so special.

Soon after she received the habit, people stopped laughing. Childeric, the King of the Franks — a remarkable nation of people who conquered that entire region of Europe and gave their name to the modern country of France — had arrived on Paris's doorstep. Childeric lay siege to the city, blockading it so that the Parisians wouldn't be able to receive food or aid. Childeric planned to starve the people to death if they didn't surrender to him and his forces.

Seeing the suffering around her, and knowing that many would die, Genevieve, with some companions, escaped the city and brought back several boatloads of food for the Parisians. It was a daring move which brought aid to the people, but it didn't change the political and military realities. Paris fell to the Franks because there was no way the city could stand against the superior Frankish forces.

On entering the city as the conqueror, Childeric, who had learned about Genevieve's daring, summoned her and listened to what she had to say. Because of Genevieve he spared many people, and he started a church in honor of Saint Denis, a bishop of Paris who had long been beloved there.

Another terrible threat arrived on the doorstep of Paris during Genevieve's lifetime, and she became even more famous for her way of handling the new peril. Attila the Hun, called "the Scourge of God," was rampaging all over Europe, terrifying people and wrecking the countryside. The Huns had come from the wastelands of Asia, and they had damaged so many Christian countries that people, mistakenly, began to think those wild barbarians were sent to punish them for their sins.

Word came that Attila was on his way to Paris with his band of marauders, and the people of the city started to pack their belongings and seek safety in other areas. Genevieve argued with the people, saying that prayers would save Paris from the terrible danger coming over the next hill.

Many, convinced that no one could be that good, laughed at Genevieve and began walking out of the city. Others, inspired by her goodness, stayed at her side and began praying.

Attila and his Huns turned away from Paris at the last moment, as Genevieve had predicted, and the city was saved. Those who had laughed came creeping back, feeling foolish, as Paris celebrated its deliverance from Attila the Hun.

Later, when Clovis became King of the Franks, with Saint Clotilde, his wife at his side, Genevieve converted him to the faith. Clovis and his court became Catholics in 496. Genevieve, worn out from her labors on behalf of Paris, died in the year 500. She was buried with honors in the church built by Clovis and Saint Clotilde. Genevieve's feast day is January 3rd.

Pope Leo the Great

Chapter 12

Pope Leo the Great

Modern popes have very definite roles to play in the world, heading the Church and meeting with people of all faiths and nationalities. In the past, however, the papacy also held political power, as did Pope Leo I, called "the Great" by historians. Born in Rome, he was educated as a priest and served two other popes, Saint Celestine I and Sixtus III. People early learned that Leo was an organized individual, with a good mind and a generous heart, and they put him to good use because then, as now, there aren't many humans like him walking around.

On one occasion Leo was sent into Gaul (modern France) to settle an argument between two Roman generals who were about to start a war over territory. Generals in those days could start wars without asking the government for permission, and they were a bit cranky about their rights and rank. Leo had to talk fast to settle the argument, but he managed to stop the feud just in time to welcome a delegation of priests and bishops arriving on his doorstep.

The men, who had come all the way from Rome, announced that the pope was dead. They informed Leo that *he* had been elected to head the Church as the new Pontiff (a Roman term used to describe the pope). These men knew, as had the two previous popes, that Leo was heaven-sent to help the Church in times of crises. Leo returned to Rome and was consecrated pope on September 29, 440.

A man of intense activity and concern, Leo I wrote, then preached sermons everywhere. Ninety-six of his sermons survive to this day. His letters are also in the Vatican archives and show his interest in life.

The Church had many problems. To handle some of these growing disputes, Leo I presided over the Council of Chalcedon, called by Emperor Marcian and attended by 600 bishops from around the known world. The pope was able to reconcile those who held different ideas about Christ and the Church, and the council ended as a success, having solved some of those difficulties.

That sense of contentment was short-lived as Attila the Hun and his fierce band arrived near Rome in 452, coming from the wastelands of Asia. People feared Attila, and the thought of hundreds of riders on horseback coming into their town intent on murder and destruction sent people fleeing in all directions.

Attila — "the Scourge of God" — and his army were camped just outside the city. The people of Rome told Pope Leo I that he was the one to meet with Attila. "Who better to face such a monster?" the people argued. If God allowed such a "Scourge" to roam the world punishing men and women for their sins, as it was commonly thought, the only human being equipped to handle him was the pope.

Accepting the challenge, Leo took Avienus, the consul (a man with an honorary position in the government), and Trigetius, the Roman governor, with him. They set out with a small group of priests who chanted litanies along the way. Attila was camped just beyond the city, in a place called Peschiera. Leo and his men sailed to the meeting on the river's edge. They sang, carried torches, and tried to control their fear. To their surprise, at the meeting they were welcomed by Attila and given his protection.

No one knows what Pope Leo I said to Attila the Hun when they came face to face, because the two men spoke in private. Whatever it was, Attila turned away from Rome immediately. He broke camp and marched the Huns and their terrible weapons in another direction. There has been a great deal of speculation about what was said, but no one knows for sure because neither Leo or Attila ever offered any information about the conversation.

The Huns had their own priests, called "shamans," and one of these supposedly had warned Attila throughout the journey about meeting a man who led an "army of the risen dead" who would punish him if he made a wrong move. Leo I not only represented the living Christians of his time, but the Communion of Saints as well, those countless martyrs and saints who were in heaven. Attila might have been alarmed at the thought of what Leo's "army" could do to him, or Leo I might have told him something that put the fear of God into the barbarian. The meeting has remained one of history's mysteries.

Returning to Rome, Leo I told the people the good news, and the city went wild with celebrations. Three years later, however, another group of barbarians arrived on Rome's doorstep, and these were men of a different breed. The Vandals, originally from northern Germany on the Baltic coast, were led by Geiseric. The Vandals were not like the Huns, who wandered about, ruining the countryside, then pushing on. The Vandals owned a good part of northern Africa at the time, and they were the leading power in the Mediterranean. Using a huge fleet of ships, they attacked the local ports at will.

Once again Pope Leo I went out to meet the newcomers. He knew he wouldn't be able to turn the Vandals aside as easily as the Huns, so he made a compromise with them instead. The Vandals could enter Rome, because there was no way of keeping them out of the city. They could spend 15 days wrecking Rome, but could not kill people or set fire to buildings. For more than two weeks the Romans watched in horror as the barbarians walked off with or ruined everything they owned, but at the end of the Vandals' visit at least they were alive.

Afterward, Leo had to refurnish the churches and help the Romans, now poor. He spent the rest of his life restoring order. Leo died on November 10, 461 after serving as the Holy Father of the world for 21 years. His relics are preserved in the Vatican basilica, and his feast day is celebrated on November 10.

Martyrs
of the Theban Legion

Chapter 13

The Martyrs
of the Theban Legion

The ancient city of Thebes, now located within the
boundaries of the town of Luxor, some 400 miles south of
modern Cairo, Egypt, is a destination for thousands of travelers
each year. Thebes contains the largest temple ever built, the
temple of Kamak, and the city served as the capital of ancient
Egypt under the Pharaohs (the ancient Egyptian name for
rulers) of the New Kingdom Period in that land, from 1550 B.C.
to 1070 B.C. The great Pharaohs, such as Tuthmosis III, Seti I,
and Ramesses II, used Thebes at least part of each year as their
royal residence and as the seat of government.

Thebes is located in the area called Upper Egypt, which is
actually south of (or below) Lower Egypt. If this sounds mixed
up, it is, but there's a reason why. Upper and Lower Egypt were
named early in the nation's history. The Nile, which is the
world's longest river, cuts through Egypt and streams some
4,665 miles on its journey through the rest of Africa.

The Nile River does not flow the way other rivers do in the
world. The Nile flows out of the heart of Africa, north to the
Mediterranean Sea. Upper Egypt was the part of the nation
closest to the source of the Nile and was named accordingly.

When the New Kingdom collapsed, Egypt was invaded by
other nations and ruled by other kings, including the Roman
emperors. Egypt became a province of the empire after Marc
Antony and Queen Cleopatra lost the Battle of Actium in 31 B.C.

and killed themselves to avoid being dragged back to Rome chained to the emperor's chariot. The Romans were known for coming up with awful punishments for enemies they captured.

By the 2nd century, the Christian faith had also taken root in Egypt, and Thebes was part of the growing Christian Church in the region. There are still many Christians in Egypt, part of the Coptic Rite, a beautiful member of the great family of Catholic liturgical traditions.

As in other provinces of the empire, the Romans recruited men from Thebes and nearby towns as warriors to be trained for service in their famed legions. The Egyptian armies had once ruled that part of the world, and were known for their cavalry units and archers. They won the original battle called Armageddon at Ar-Megiddo, the fortress in the pass near Mount Carmel. The Romans, aware of the Egyptians' abilities, sought them out and found willing recruits in Thebes and elsewhere, as Roman military service offered several rewards. Many of these recruits came from the old capital of Egypt, and the unit that was made up of these men was named after Thebes.

The Legion of Thebes had some outstanding officers as well, named Maurice, Exuperius, and Candidus, all Christians. Maurice and his officer companions shared everything with their men, including the Christian faith.

The Theban legion received many Roman honors in its military history, serving in Roman imperial wars of conquest and in the ongoing battles against barbarian tribes that rebelled against Roman rule and Roman taxes. A barbarian rebellion began in A.D. 287, and co-emperor Maximian (ruling with Emperor Diocletian), a pagan who worshipped the god Hercules especially, called on the Legion of Thebes and other units under his command to launch an assault.

The barbarians, a tribe from Gaul (which is now modern France), were located on the Rhone River and were ferocious warriors, particularly when they were defending their homelands against an enemy. The Romans faced terrible threats from the barbarians, who fought by ambushing and sneaking up on legions which were careless enough to be led astray into an unknown wilderness.

The Legion of Thebes, alongside other Roman units, fought well under the emperor and proved victorious. The barbarians were taken prisoner or killed, and Roman rule was again secure in the region. Maximian decided to hold a great celebration for his troops, starting with pagan rituals that would honor the ancient gods. He considered it the proper thing to do and had no idea that anyone in his legionary forces would have objections. Perhaps Maximian had been shielded from the changes in the empire, or perhaps he just didn't care what lesser-ranked people thought. The old ways of Rome were good enough for him, and he had the power to make his will known and obeyed.

Maximian started the festivities in good spirits, calling on every member of the legions in his command to sacrifice to the gods of Rome, whom he believed had granted victory to him in the face of an enemy. The sacrifices usually involved throwing a pinch of salt on an altar, giving praise, sprinkling incense, or kneeling before a statue. It was going to be a grand celebration, and as he sat on his portable throne he was content to have his men parade before him and the old deities of the empire.

To Maximian's surprise, however, when the Legion of Thebes was called on to start the sacrifices, the unit loudly refused, to a man. Not one grain of salt nor one whiff of incense would be offered by these soldiers, and they had no intention of even nodding their heads at a pagan god. To make their point, and to ensure that everyone understood how they felt, the Theban Legion withdrew from the main camp and set up their tents some distance away. Not only did they refuse to take part, they made it clear that they were Christians who didn't even want to see the pagan ceremonies, no matter how glorious Maximian felt they were.

Enraged by the refusal because he was a pious pagan and because his imperial will was being challenged, Maximian marched on the Theban Legion camp and demanded that the men sacrifice to the gods. He told them they were foolish to defy him because he represented everything that Rome stood for. The men of the Legion, encouraged by Maurice and the other officers, still refused to salute pagan idols.

Maximian had to act quickly because this challenge could weaken his support among the other units in his command. He gathered the remaining legions and surrounded the Theban camp, demanding that the Thebans put aside their pride and accept him as emperor and as commander.

He lined up the members of the Theban Legion, ordering one last time that they follow him to the altars of the old gods of Rome. The sight of the men falling into line must have sent shivers up and down the spines of their military comrades. These were veterans of combat who knew what kinds of punishment could be handed to them by an emperor. The fact that they accepted their fate and stood in line for the coming blows impressed their companions, men who lived and died in battles, and held honor and pride as virtues among fighting men.

Maximian threatened once more, but his words faded in the air as the Theban men stood firm before him. He then announced that every 10th man in the Legion of Thebes would be executed if they did not obey him. Maximian was not obeyed, and the threat was made good. The legionnaires watched in shock and horror as one tenth of the unit was struck down. To the veteran warriors on the scene, the unnecessary deaths of trained soldiers was an ugly, brutal display. To those who were newer in the legions, the shock of seeing Romans murdering Romans made them question how brave they would be in the same circumstances.

Maurice and the other Theban officers urged the men to stand firm, and they refused Maximian's commands and watched their comrades in Christ fall as martyrs for the faith.

Then one legionnaire from Thebes announced: "We have seen our comrades killed. We do not mourn them but rejoice at the honor done to them."

Maximian became even more furious, knowing that he had risked a great deal on this demonstration of his power. The men were idiots, he believed, but they could hurt him with their Christian view of martyrdom as an honor. Angry, Maximian gave an order to the other units present. He had the *entire* Legion of Thebes slain.

Maximian and all the powers of the imperial throne of Rome could not stop the fire of Christian faith that was storming across the world. Maurice and the Legion of Thebes were killed and left in the fields of Gaul, but the story of their martyrdom swept across the Roman provinces as the veteran soldiers of the remaining legions spoke of them around campfires and in the shadows of the night. The Thebans had died, but they lived in memory, and their countrymen in Upper Egypt on the Nile wept, prayed, and rejoiced that so many of their own had gained the crown of martyrdom of the Church.

Standing firm for Christ, even dying for him, may seem rash in this age of compromise. Many modern people, when faced with a similar situation would have to talk to their friends, ask others what they think, write letters to newspaper columnists for advice, or appear on TV talk shows before they got around to making up their minds. The men of the Legion of Thebes had no self-doubts, no lack of courage or faith. It was simple to their minds. They had sworn to follow Christ, and like the warriors they were, they walked the extra mile, the most painful one, in Christ's service.

Because of men like this, the Church began to overcome the madness, evils, and cruelty of the ancient world. Because they were willing to die, the Church lived. Maurice and his valiant companions were named martyrs of the faith and canonized. In some books they are listed as the Legion of Thebes, in others as Saint Maurice and Companions. Their feast day is September 22nd.

Mary Magdalene

Chapter 14

Mary Magdalene

One of the most fascinating women in the New Testament of the Holy Bible is Mary Magdalene, a woman no one really knows very well, even though the Christian world hears about her courage and devotion each year as part of the Passion of Christ — the Easter story. For example, no one is sure about her name, her identity, or even where she was buried.

That Mary Magdalene was blessed by God is shown in the Bible in a number of ways: she stood beside the Virgin Mary at the foot of the cross; Jesus defended her at the banquet; and later appeared to her in the garden after his resurrection. Her mysterious story, as told in the New Testament, remains exciting and inspiring to each new generation of Christians.

She was called Mary Magdalene or Mary Magdala, and the last part of her name could have been taken from her possible birthplace, Magdala, a small town on the western shore of Lake Galilee. The name may also have come from the ancient Hebraic term for "curling women's hair," as she is traditionally shown with long hair. That particular hairstyle, wearing her hair unbound and uncovered, marked her as what the modern world would call a "tramp." Decent God-fearing women covered their hair with a veil and wore sensible robes and shawls. Any woman dressed without a veil was considered a bad woman who was advertising the fact that she had loose morals.

Mary Magdalene has been identified with many other women in the New Testament, including Mary, the sister of

Lazarus (raised from the dead by Jesus), but there's no conclusive evidence to prove these theories about her real position, family, or rank. Several countries also claim that she was in their region after the Ascension of Christ, and two separate sites are listed as tombs of at least part of her remains.

What is known is that Mary Magdalene appeared at a banquet to wash with her tears the feet of Christ and to anoint his feet with expensive oils. The other people at the banquet, mostly men, were horrified by Mary Magdalene's appearance at the house. Women like her were not welcomed in the homes of God-fearing decent folk, because their presence allowed other people in the neighborhood to spread rumors.

The guests at the party began to wonder out loud why Jesus, who was so pure and sacred, would allow himself to be touched by someone like her, an act which, according to old traditions, contaminated him. None of the other guests would allow Mary Magdalene to even approach them, let alone wash their feet!

Jesus, hearing their concerns, answered that when he arrived at the house for the banquet, having been invited by the host, no one had followed the customary tradition of washing the dust from his feet. People worried about things like that in those days. This woman, who wept over her past sins, offered him and God the Father the most beautiful gift of all, a contrite heart; a heart that was filled with awareness of sin and its deadly effects.

Later, when Christ was taken by the Romans and condemned to death, Mary Magdalene stood at the foot of the Cross, unafraid. Except for Saint John, the other Apostles and the many followers of Christ had quickly disappeared when they realized they could get into trouble with the Roman authorities for knowing Jesus. Peter, upon whom Christ would build his Church, three times denied that he knew Jesus in front of a group of people, as the Master had predicted.

The Romans and the local people sneered at Mary Magdalene for keeping watch at the crucifixion, but she paid no attention to them. In the past she had been laughed at and chased out of town by her neighbors for doing bad things, so why should she be upset now, when she was defending the Christ?

Jesus was dying on the cross, and there was nothing else in the entire world that mattered to her. That singleness of vision marks Mary Magdalene throughout the New Testament. When Christ came into her life everything else faded out of view for her. Nothing kept her from following Christ or from defending him and his mother.

Mary Magdalene stood beside Mary, the Mother of Christ, comforting her, until Jesus died on the cross. She then helped the Christian followers who arrived to take Jesus' body from the cross to the tomb of Joseph of Arimathea, a prominent Jewish scholar and businessman. That tomb, prepared by Joseph for his own burial, was given freely so that Jesus would be entombed with honors according to the old traditions.

There Mary Magdalene and other women prepared the remains for burial, wrapping Jesus' body in fresh linens and anointing it with oils. At that time in the world, there were no funeral homes. Relatives and friends took care of the preparations themselves.

On the third day following the burial, Mary Magdalene and other women arrived with more linens and oils, fulfilling the custom of freshening the corpse over a certain period of time. When the women arrived at the tomb, however, they found the soldiers sent to guard the body of Christ lying fast asleep. The great stone that had been placed across the entrance to the tomb was on one side of the opening, no longer blocking the way.

That the guards were sleeping on duty didn't upset Mary Magdalene. The sight of the stone moved from the entrance, however, alarmed her because she was frightened by what might have happened. She ran into the tomb to find Jesus' body, because that was all that mattered to her, and it seemed obvious to her that someone or something had gone into the tomb, perhaps with an evil purpose.

Inside, Mary Magdalene saw an angel sitting on the empty slab of stone where Christ had been lain. She did not faint at the sight of him, and she did not scream. She asked where the authorities had taken Christ's remains. The angel answered her, asking, why she would look for Jesus in a tomb, when he had been raised.

After hearing that, and seeing the evidence that Jesus was gone from the tomb, the women ran to where the Apostles were hiding in fear, and announced that Jesus was risen from the grave. Because of this, Mary Magdalene has been called "the apostle to the Apostles." She then returned to the garden alone, not content to take even the word of an angel when it came to finding out where Jesus was.

As Mary watched over the tomb, Jesus appeared to her in his risen state. Although she didn't recognize him at first, she realized who it was when he spoke to her. Mary called him *Rabboni*, a word meaning "teacher" in Aramaic, the language of the time. Mary knelt before Christ, feeling "fear and great joy" (as the Bible explains it), and she honored him and praised God for the resurrection of her Master.

In time, Jesus appeared to others he was close to, and the world knows well the story of the Resurrection and the Ascension, and the founding of the Church at Pentecost. Mary Magdalene appears to have become part of the missionary efforts of the new Church, and several places claim that she lived and died among their people.

English tradition states that Mary Magdalene arrived in the British Isles with Joseph of Arimathea, and certain places are still called by the name given to them during Joseph's time. Constantinople, now Istanbul, in modern Turkey, claims that Mary's relics were taken to the city in 886. Her tomb was found in France in 1600, however, when a new convent was being constructed at a site listed in old records as Le Sainte Baume. During the French Revolution these relics were vandalized, and only the skull of this courageous woman remains in its original burial site. Her feast day is July 22.

John Neumann

Chapter 15

John Neumann

When the Catholic Church started expanding its missionary and parish work in America after the Revolutionary War, many Europeans came to serve in the priesthood and in educational and hospital programs. All kinds of highly trained people came to the new country to offer their help in spreading the faith. The Church needed all of these volunteers, especially those who spoke the languages of the immigrants to the New World, and the local bishops of the dioceses welcomed them with open arms.

One of these volunteers was a man named John Nepomucen Neumann, who was from Bohemia (formerly a kingdom, then a province of the country once known as Czechoslovakia) where he was born on March 28, 1811. His parents were of German and Czech decent, and he had a gift for languages, having learned them in his youth at home. Actually, John Neumann spoke seven major languages, as well as the ancient tongues of Latin, Greek, and Hebrew, and he could make himself understood in the many and various Slavic dialects of his homeland. Later, when he was ministering to the Irish immigrants in his diocese in America, he learned Gaelic as well, so the Irish would feel more at home in their religious services. John Neumann was also a gifted botanist, having studied that natural science for many years, and he was considered somewhat of an expert in the field.

John entered the seminary in Bohemia in 1831. He was interested in missionary work and accepted an assignment in

America, landing in the young nation in 1836. Bishop Dubois of New York ordained him on June 25th of that year, then sent him to western New York, where he served as a pastor for four years in a parish in a farming district. As more and more people arrived in the United States, the Church had to start parishes for them and their families.

In 1840, John Neumann entered the Redemptorist Congregation, a famous religious group founded in 1732 in Italy by Saint Alphonsus Ligouri, dedicated to bringing the faith to the poor. Father Neumann became the first professed member of this congregation in America in 1842. In time he would become the local superior, then the Vice-Provincial, or assistant superior, of the entire congregation in the United States.

His abilities, however, didn't go unnoticed by the Catholic leaders outside of the Redemptorists, and the local Church authorities believed that this educated, outstanding man had to assume greater responsibilities for the good of all. He was named the bishop of Philadelphia, but he refused the position until Pope Pius IX gave him a direct order to accept it.

Certain Catholics were scandalized by the appointment of John Neumann to the position of bishop of Philadelphia. They complained he was a foreigner who spoke with an accent, who was more at home with peasants and farm workers than with people of wealth and rank in society. They believed that the Church needed a polished man, someone who could charm the people of other faiths at parties and teas. John Neumann, they claimed, was educated and skilled with languages, but there was a no-nonsense air about him that didn't fit in with the high and mighty of society.

Some of these enemies of John Neumann visited other high-ranking Catholic clergymen to voice their opinions. They didn't realize how shallow they were in their views. The Church didn't need someone who knew how to sip tea. The Church needed a shepherd of souls.

Because some of the enemies of John Neumann were powerful individuals, their arguments were heard courteously by Church officials. However, their complaints weren't strong enough to stop his appointment.

Bishop Neumann knew what the socialites of Philadelphia were saying about him. Possibly these people felt threatened by John Neumann. He didn't come from an old Philadelphia family, and couldn't claim that his ancestors arrived on the *Mayflower*, but he was proving his intelligence and closeness to God, and that made others work to hurt him.

Even in the face of opposition, he accepted the assignment as the bishop of Philadelphia when the pope told him to. He was consecrated and began his work, concerned with the number of new families in the area and the need for decent schools. Bishop Neumann brought in several congregations of teaching brothers and sisters from European cities, started 50 new parishes, and worked on the new cathedral for Philadelphia.

Knowing that many Catholics were uneducated in the faith, he wrote two catechisms in 1852. These catechisms were so beautiful, so filled with knowledge, and written in plain words that made sense, that they were adopted by other dioceses throughout the country over the next years. Bishop Neumann might not be welcomed in the fancy homes of Philadelphia, but he was considered a Godsend by others who had the care of souls entrusted to them.

Bishop Neumann built almost 100 parochial schools in the diocese. He and other pioneering bishops in America were always aware of the need for schools, which became the pride and joy of Catholics in America and ensured each new generation of a decent education in the faith, as well as in the changing sciences and arts.

He worried about the priests serving in the new parishes, knowing that some of them had little or no training before they started their missionary work. He intended to make sure that future Catholic leaders would be better trained. Bishop

Neumann insisted on setting new standards of scholarship and studies in the local seminary. He also established preparatory programs (before a man entered the seminary) for candidates to the priesthood.

Slowly, everyone — rich and poor — began to appreciate the man God had given them. He watched over all of his projects until the last moment that God allowed him to spend on the earth. Bishop John Neumann simply dropped dead in the streets of Philadelphia while making his usual rounds of parish visitations. He died on January 5, 1860.

His remains are in Saint Peter's Redemptorist Church in Philadelphia, which has become a shrine to his memory. He was canonized in 1977 by Pope Paul VI, and his feast day is January 5th.

Pope Pius X

Chapter 16

Pope Pius X

The world has been blessed with some remarkable popes in recent decades, sent by God and destined to take care of the Church in a time of particular need. Certainly, modern times have been periods of nuttiness with wars, political unrest, riots and revolutions, as our TV news programs remind us daily.

One of the popes who lived at the beginning of the modern age was Saint Pius X. He not only led the Church through difficult times and changing political scenes in his own time, but he continues to influence the lives of people today. He deserves the thanks of millions because of his intense love for the Blessed Sacrament, and his desire for all Catholics to share It.

He was born Giuseppe Sarto in 1835, in the little town of Riese, Italy. Always believing himself destined for the Church, he was ordained at age 23, then assigned as a pastor, a post he held for 17 years. These years of parish service, of personal contact with Catholic families and their hopes and dreams, gave Father Sarto a very special insight into the Church and its role among ordinary people, and he used that experience in his later years when he held the great power of the Vatican.

In 1884 he was named the bishop of Mantua, then was given the rank of Cardinal and made the Patriarch (the Archbishop) of Venice. Already he was noted for "angelic kindness." This means that he respected the rights of all other individuals and never showed impatience or anger, even in the face of stubborn arguments. Pope Pius X deserves sainthood just for remaining calm when so many others were racing around in panic!

When Pope Leo XIII died in 1903, the Cardinals of the Church, the highest-ranking members of the clergy from around the world, gathered in what is called a Conclave. This Conclave (or College of Cardinals) is designed to allow the Cardinals to meet away from the prying eyes of the world, and elect a new Pontiff (the Roman term used to describe the pope). In the Conclave following the death of Pope Leo XIII, the College of Cardinals elected Cardinal Rampolla del Tindaro as the new Pontiff. Before he could be installed, however, Emperor Franz Josef II of Austria, a powerful ruler of the period, vetoed that election.

Nowadays it seems strange that a king or emperor could tell the Church what to do. Some people at the time didn't think it was a good idea, either, but that was the way things were at the time. Certain rulers — like that of Austria — claimed the right to have a voice in the election of a pope, because the Church was allowed to have an official role in their countries' governments. In earlier history, the rulers of some countries didn't hesitate to *kidnap* the popes who disagreed with them, and imprisoned those they didn't think would follow their royal instructions. This had changed by the time Pope Leo XIII died, and rulers could only use their veto vote to show their disapproval.

Horrified by the veto, the Cardinals wanted to fight against Emperor Franz Josef, who was a very determined individual who would not hesitate to use force to carry out his will. In order to avoid a confrontation, Cardinal Rampolla del Tindaro refused to accept the papacy and urged his fellow Cardinals to find someone else. They then elected Giuseppe Sarto, the Patriarch of Venice, who took the name Pius X.

Looking back it's easy to see the Hand of God in this choice, although Emperor Franz Josef was probably not thinking about God's Will when he put in his veto. The Emperor was an ambitious man who was anxious to maintain his empire and didn't want someone in charge of the Church who might cause him difficulty. Actually, Franz Josef and leaders like him were doomed by the changing political scenes of the world, but he didn't know that at the time. The emperor didn't know too much about the new pope, who said: "I was born poor, I have lived poor, and I want to die poor." This man had been placed by God in the glorious surroundings of the Vatican, but the art and beauty didn't change him. First, he had lived too long to be impressed by sudden fame and power. Also, he remembered the poor families of his parish from his younger days, and he knew that everything a person could own in the world was only temporary.

Pius X started his reign by issuing a decree that Franz Josef and other rulers no longer had any right to interfere in the decisions of the Church. Franz Josef took it well, perhaps because he saw the first signs of change coming and decided to bow out gracefully.

The pope began to educate the people of the world about the dangers of "modernism," a point of view where every generation believes that it alone has the answers to problems without having to learn from the mistakes of the past. Pius X's great encyclical (an official letter written by the pope) concerning modernism and its ideas talked of the Church being involved in an effort "to renew all things in Christ."

He revised the law of the Church (a series of rules and regulations called Canon Law) and regulated the liturgy (the celebration of the Mass) throughout the world. The pope was trying to make people understand that they can't change things just for the sake of change. He founded the Biblical Institute, which was designed to allow scholars to study the past and to teach others about Christ and the historical Church without allowing people to rewrite history to suit their personal ambitions.

Emperor Franz Josef was having problems of his own. His son and heir, Rudolf, killed himself, and his second heir, Archduke Ferdinand, was assassinated by a terrorist; an act that started World War I in June, 1914. On August 20th of that year, Pope Pius X, who had developed severe bronchitis as a result of his grief over the outbreak of the war, died.

His life was a remarkable one, and he served the Church beautifully during his reign. He is remembered by us today for these contributions and more. Pius X was devoted to the Holy Eucharist and the Blessed Sacrament, and believed that people the world over should understand the great privilege of receiving Holy Communion.

Over the centuries the idea of receiving Holy Communion had gone through a series of changes. Until the early part of this century, most people received Communion only once or twice a year, *if* they were considered good enough to approach the altar. Even the great saints had to ask permission to receive Christ in the Holy Eucharist. Pius X believed that men and women should be allowed to receive Christ every day, if they attended Mass and were living as Christ commanded. He also lowered the age for First Holy Communion in order to allow the young to unite themselves to Christ in this great sacrament.

Because of Pope Pius X, everyone can receive Holy Communion in our parish Masses, and everyone can keep vigil over the Blessed Sacrament on the altars of the Church. He was canonized as a saint by Pope Pius XII, and his feast day is August 21.

Edith Stein

Chapter 17

Edith Stein

Once in a great while, someone is born with a brilliant mind and a sense of honor and truth. They are rare, but can influence others by their lives and God-given talents. Such a woman was Edith Stein, who was born in Breslau, Germany, on October 12, 1891. She was the seventh child of a prosperous Jewish family of Breslau, raised in the Jewish faith, showing absolute brilliance even in childhood.

When she entered the university, she was taught by the great masters of philosophy, and began to be well known among academic (school-related) people in Germany. Edith abandoned her Jewish faith in 1904, announcing that she had become an atheist, because the philosophy that she had studied taught that God did not exist. People in every age of the world have invented such theories, even though the old wisdom teaches: "Only the fool says in his heart there is no God." Since Edith Stein was nobody's fool, she would soon change her mind.

Edith was intelligent and could take opposing ideas and put them together in a logical way that made sense. Most people have enough trouble keeping one set of ideas in their heads. Edith was able to learn two or three philosophies (sets of principles and theories about how life works) and keep them straight, even weaving them together to form conclusions. Her academic career was well on its way when she began teaching at the University of Freiburg, and everyone expected great things from her.

Edith Stein, however, was not a woman who would deny truth when she discovered it staring her in the face. She was also a woman who would not deny the obvious, once she understood what was taking place. Almighty God was about to show her the truth of the Catholic faith, knowing she would respond with honor and with a generous heart. This soul was chosen by him for a special role.

While visiting in Bavaria in the autumn of 1921, Edith Stein picked up a book on the life of Saint Teresa of Ávila, the great Catholic mystic who was given the rank of Doctor of the Church. She was so astounded by what she read in the book that she began to study the Church, reading books and catechisms to learn about the Catholic faith. Edith was serious in her study. She was quite capable of reading and understanding the great theologians of the faith, and she took care to read their works closely and give them an honest opportunity to present their case before her open mind.

On January 1, 1922, as a result of reading and studying, and of God's grace, Edith Stein was baptized a Catholic. From that day on she was a daily communicant, receiving the Holy Eucharist at early morning Masses. Her sister, Rosa, also became a Catholic. Their conversions upset people throughout Germany. They didn't understand how the two women could turn their backs on everything they had known. Edith Stein kept silent when they argued with her, and she continued her work and faith. She would surprise her former friends even more, because she knew that God was calling her to the Carmelite cloister, to the Order founded by Saint Teresa of Ávila so many centuries before.

On April 15, 1934, Edith Stein received the habit (the official robes) of the Carmelites in Cologne, Germany, becoming a cloistered nun and taking the name Benedicta of the Cross. She took her perpetual vows a few years later, content that she had come home in the spirit, brought to Christ by the truth of the Christian faith.

But life was changing in Germany. The life of an individual was no longer important. Sinister forces that would one day involve the entire world in a terrible war and bring about untold human suffering and death were taking control.

In 1937, the synagogues of Cologne were burned by the Nazis (the German national party led by Adolf Hitler) who were spreading terrible propaganda — that is, lies — about the Jewish people. The Nazis were using their power to force the German people to hate the Jewish people and their beliefs. Using speeches, radio shows, and newspapers, the Nazis told the German people only one side of every story or event. Jewish people didn't have a chance to defend themselves.

The Catholic authorities, seeing what was happening around them and worried about Edith Stein and Rosa (who hadn't become a nun but was a devout Catholic), transferred them to the Carmelite convent at Echt in Holland. They believed the two women would be safe there from the Nazi evil that was controlling Germany and its citizens.

Edith wrote two books, *Finite and Eternal Being* and *The Science of the Cross*, while in the convent in Holland, and they are brilliant, deep, spiritual works that continue to influence scholars and theologians. The superior of the convent asked her to make use of the intelligence God had given her in the service of others. Her books are not easy to read because they are full of complicated ideas, but they are a real contribution to the faith on a scholarly level.

Meanwhile, the Nazis had invaded Holland and started new persecutions of the Jews. Having rounded up and murdered all the known Jewish people in Europe (called the Holocaust), the Nazis began a new program. Hitler ordered that all Jews who had converted to Christianity be disposed of in the concentration camps. Their conversions to the faith meant nothing in Hitler's eyes.

That Edith Stein was a holy soul, gifted by God and interested only in the work of salvation, didn't matter to the

Nazis. Her intellect, her soul, and her spirit of truth held no meaning to them.

The Nazis entered the Carmelite cloister on August 2, 1942, arresting the Stein sisters. They were taken to Auschwitz concentration camp, which was only 20 miles from Breslau, Edith's childhood home.

Both Edith and Rosa Stein were murdered in Auschwitz by the Nazis on August 9th or 10th, 1942. Marched into the gas chamber, they died and were burned in the ovens designed to cremate bodies.

Edith Stein is now called Blessed by the Church, having been beatified by Pope John Paul II in 1987 when he visited West Germany, as it was known before the fall of the Berlin Wall. Her feast day is August 10.

Thérèse of Lisieux

Chapter 18

Thérèse of Lisieux, the Little Flower

On September 30, 1897, a very young Carmelite nun died after a long, painful illness in the convent of Lisieux, France. Some of the older nuns in that religious community were preparing a booklet about her life, to be sent to other Carmelite convents. They were a little confused about what they could say about the dead nun. The sisters asked one another what they could possibly tell others about her, because, as one of them explained it: "She never did anything to speak of." The young nun was the Little Flower, Saint Thérèse, who would become the patroness of the Church's world missions.

It seems a bit strange that the Carmelite nuns living with the Little Flower were so blind that they missed the fact that a saint was living among them. It seems odd that Thérèse's holiness could be overlooked by women who themselves were dedicated to the spiritual life and to perfection. But there are reasons why this happened.

First, this particular Carmelite convent may have been filled with genuine rare souls, women who lived the rule perfectly, accepting prayer, penance, and the spirit of "being alone with the Alone" as their way of life. Even a future saint could get lost in such a house, particularly a very young one who kept silent and used flowery Victorian terms to write about her spiritual experiences.

The Victorian Age, named after Queen Victoria of England, was a time of opposites. Amid an era of terrible wars, people avoided reality by speaking in poetic terms about it. Nothing ugly or bad was mentioned, and everything was described in lovely words and images. Thérèse was a true Victorian in her speech and writing, as she had been taught. She used pretty words to describe some of her most severe spiritual trials, like exhaustion, loneliness, or doubts, hiding them in flowery words. Some people today have a hard time understanding what she was talking about because her words are so poetic.

Don't be fooled because she was a teenager and a product of the Victorian age. Underneath the pretty words, the poetic images, and flowery phrases, one of the strongest human hearts that ever lived can be seen. She was a true Friend of God, granted special graces, and she was not weak. She wrote about her life only in beautiful words, but she dared to risk everything to meet the spiritual standards set for her by God. She died in the process of becoming truly whole and perfect.

Secondly, the vocation of the Carmelite nuns, even today, involves hours in the chapel, kneeling on bare floors, working alone in their rooms or other areas, not talking, not eating meat, and (during the penitential seasons of the year, such as Lent and Advent) living without eggs, butter, cheese, and other dairy foods. The nuns meet twice a day for recreation. The evening hour is a time of work, and the nuns bring their knitting, sewing, painting, or other task into the recreational room.

The Carmelites don't sit around complaining, nor do they think that they are the only people in the world who care. Most Carmels have marvelously balanced communities, made up of women from rich and poor backgrounds, some with intelligence or artistic ability, others with good common sense.

Now Thérèse, a teenager, fitted into that world easily. Her community sisters found her sweet, gentle, kind, helpful, and filled with holy thoughts, all of which described a good Carmelite. She didn't tell the other sisters that she was receiving special favors and trials in prayer, so they had no way of knowing what she was going through. Thérèse didn't hold her audiences spellbound with revelations, nor did she chat about her spiritual life. She was a good Carmelite, in a convent full of women dedicated to the same ideals.

Thérèse's life didn't start out with any extraordinary signs of her special role in the world, either. She was born on January 2, 1873, the youngest child of Louis and Azélie-Marie Martin, in the town of Alençon, France. In 1877, Thérèse's mother died, and the family moved to Lisieux. There Louis Martin and his daughters were looked after by an aunt, although Thérèse was raised and educated by her sisters: Marie, Pauline, and Celine.

Quick and bright, she had a close relationship with her father, who favored her, perhaps because she was the youngest. Tradition tells that one night while they were out walking together, Thérèse pointed to the sky and the stars, saying that she would shine there in time because she was destined to become a saint. Whatever her father thought, he continued to protect and guide her, and their family life was normal and happy.

When Thérèse was nine years old, her sister Pauline entered the Carmelite convent in Lisieux. Thérèse missed her, but she watched Pauline receive the habit of the Carmelites and knew that she belonged in Carmel too. Her sister, Marie, became the second member of the family to enter the Lisieux Carmel soon after, and Thérèse began to ask for permission to join them there. Of course, the local bishop had no intention of allowing it. Although he admired Thérèse's belief that she was called to the Carmelites, he felt she was too young.

Thérèse obeyed the bishop's wishes. During a visit to the Vatican in Rome with her father, however, Thérèse had the opportunity to kneel before the Holy Father, Pope Leo XIII, to receive his personal blessing. Normally, people are asked to keep silent when they meet the pope, because he has more to do than listen to complaints. Thérèse, however, then only 14, broke the rule and asked for permission to enter Carmel. Pope Leo XIII was impressed by her devotion, but said that her bishop in

Lisieux had the final say. That permission was given when Thérèse was 15. On April 9, 1888, Thérèse received the habit of the Carmelites.

The following year, tragedy struck the Martin family. Louis, their father, became very ill and had to be hospitalized. A stroke affected his mental ability, and there was little that could be done for him. Louis died after several years of suffering. Celine, who had stayed at home to care for Louis, then entered Carmel as well. Four daughters of Louis and Azélie-Marie Martin were in the same convent.

In Carmel, one of Thérèse's favorite duties was to pray for missionary priests who worked in the Church's overseas missions. The Carmelites believe they can offer themselves to God, who will give graces for those men and women who are working in the mission field. Over the centuries, missionaries have depended on the prayers of the Carmelites and other contemplative, cloistered religious men and women. By living away from the world, working and praying, they become sources of grace and faith for those in the active work of the Church.

Thérèse wanted to be a missionary nun, and was invited by the Carmelite convent in Hanoi (now Ho Chi Minh City in modern Vietnam) to join them in their cloister. But before she could accept the invitation, Thérèse heard Christ, her "Bridegroom," coming to take her home to heaven. In 1896 Thérèse became ill, coughing up blood, and she knew she was dying.

Throughout her short life as a Carmelite, Thérèse had followed the daily schedule and performed all of the duties and penances, although she wasn't allowed to fast because of her age. The prioresses of the convent, women elected by the other nuns to serve as superiors of the house, weren't fooled by Thérèse's age or physical weakness. They showed their appreciation of her spiritual abilities in several ways. For example, she was appointed as the assistant novice mistress, which meant that she taught the new young women who had come to Carmel about the rule and spirit of the Order.

In June, 1897, Thérèse was placed in the infirmary (clinic), and she stayed there through her illness. She died on September 30, 1897, surrounded by her Carmelite sisters.

The booklet that was being prepared for the other Carmels of the world would have been rather brief, considering Thérèse's few years in Carmel and her outward normal, simple religious lifestyle. But there was another written record, in Thérèse's own hand. One of the prioresses, sensing that a deeply holy and beautiful spiritual life was being formed within the young woman by Almighty God, had requested that Thérèse write about her life. That booklet, called *The History of a Soul*, was sent out to other Carmels and to Church officials after she died.

Within the pages of this booklet are some of the deepest, most beautiful descriptions of spiritual life ever written. Teenaged Thérèse was a truly gifted individual, whom God instructed in the way of perfection. The key word to everything that Thérèse experienced is "love." She learned and taught that it doesn't matter how great or how small a human being is in the world, what great works you accomplish for Christ and the Church — all that matters is how much love is put into each act, each word, each thought, no matter how large or small.

By doing the normal, natural things one is expected to do, with praise and love for God, a person can make all activities works of grace and perfection. Love does not need long words or brave deeds. Love can grow in every human heart that recognizes the beauty of God and the eternal joys that the Heavenly Father has prepared for those who become his Friends.

Thérèse of Lisieux was a like a child, an innocent young woman who spent her life hidden from the world. After her death all that she knew and believed came into bloom. Miracles took place, and people found themselves weeping over the beauty of her life and soul. She was canonized by Pope Pius XI in 1925, and in 1927 was proclaimed the patroness of her beloved world missions, alongside the great missionary, Saint Francis Xavier. She is also a special patroness of all works of the faith in Russia, which may account for the stunning changes that took place there.

Thomas
the Doubting Apostle

Chapter 19

Thomas the Doubting Apostle

Thomas has been known through the centuries for his stubbornness and for his very human need to see and touch Jesus before he could believe in his resurrection. In the Bible, Thomas is also called "Didymus," a Greek name; in Aramaic, the language of Jesus' time, Thomas means "twin."

The Bible is vague about where Thomas came from, and what he did before becoming an Apostle is not known, either. The men who wrote the New Testament might have known, but it's not mentioned, perhaps because Thomas's really important work was as a disciple, called by Jesus to walk with him in his ministry.

Thomas, along with the other Apostles, disappeared after Jesus was taken prisoner by the Roman authorities. The Apostles spent several days trying to stay invisible, for they were frightened that if the Romans discovered they had known Jesus, they too would be crucified.

Then word came of Jesus' resurrection, and Thomas made his famous statement: "Unless I see the nail prints in his hands and put my finger into the wounds and my hand into his side, I will not believe." Thomas wouldn't believe what he couldn't see.

Christ appeared again several days later, however, and told Thomas: "Put your finger here and see my hands, and bring your hand and put it in my side, and do not be unbelieving, but believe." Thomas found himself touching the wounds of Christ while the other Apostles looked on. Convinced, he called out: "My Lord and my God." Jesus said: "Thomas, because you have seen me you believe. Blessed are they who have not seen and have believed." Some people, remembering Jesus' words that he would return, knew in their heart and soul without proof; others, like Thomas, needed proof that Jesus lived.

Accounts of Thomas's missionary work for the Church vary from record to record. According to the most accepted records of his apostolate he preached in India. That vast, exotic land was a long way from his home, but somehow Thomas found his way there. The "Acta Thomae" (the Acts of Thomas) dates to the 3rd century in India, where he was called Judas Thomas. Some historians believe that he went to the court of Gondophernes (also called Guduphare) around A.D. 46, one of the many royal houses in the ancient world of the East at the time.

There he earned his title as patron of architects. When asked to build a palace for the ruler, Thomas used all the money given to him for the project to help the poor. Asked why he had done such a thing, Thomas explained that mercy for the poor builds stronger foundations and futures than all the fine palaces in the world. He had to leave town rather quickly after that!

Thomas went to the coast of Malabar in India. The Syriac Christians there claim that he founded their rite and centuries-old faith. Thomas is known to have established 12 churches in the area.

Later, he had arguments with the local religious leaders, who didn't support his ministry. Thomas was martyred for the Christian faith. He was killed in a suburban area of Madras, at a site called the Big Hill. When Portuguese explorers visited Malabar in 1522, they found Thomas's tomb and heard the history of his missionary work. His relics were taken from India, and eventually moved to Ortona in Italy. Thomas's feast day is July 3rd.

John Baptist Vianney

Chapter 20

John Baptist Vianney

The saints in this book are outstanding individuals — men and women who led unusual lives and changed the world in which they lived with their energy and vision. The Church is the true Mother of all of these people, and has cared for and loved some of the greatest minds in history.

What about people with average intelligence, with average courage and ambitions? Where do ordinary people fit into God's plan? The last two saints in this book are proof that men and women of all social standings and all degrees of knowledge and position can become the Friends of God, leaving behind them traditions of faith. These two saints, in fact, might be called patrons of the average person, because one was a parish priest who couldn't do schoolwork very well, and the other was a maid in a merchant's household. They were both peasants from simple farm families, and they didn't travel all over the world to defend the faith or fight dragons or lead great armies. Both of them stayed close to the villages of their birth.

The first of these saints is John Baptist Vianney, known today as the Curé of Ars and called Jean-Baptist Vianney in the French language. (The name Curé was used by the French as a title for a parish priest.) John Vianney was born in 1786 in a small town called Dardilly, near the French city of Lyon. Not a good student, he barely passed his classes in elementary school and was really poor at Latin, which, unfortunately, was the official language of the Church at the time. A future bishop,

Matthias Loras, helped him study Latin and kept him in the classroom, where they studied for the priesthood.

Napoleon and his armies were conquering Europe, and John Vianney's seminary studies were interrupted by a call to France's military campaigns. But he missed leaving his hometown with the other recruits taken from the area, so he set out to find them. He had a guide to help him, but instead of leading John to his hometown miliary unit, he was led to a village which was a hideout for French Army deserters!

The guide couldn't believe that anyone would *want* to find a battlefield. Since John had escaped military service, the guide thought he was doing John a favor by giving him a place to hide from Napoleon's recruiters. The guide didn't think about John's family or personal honor. Once in the town, John Vianney discovered that he was needed by the local children, so he stayed, sending word to his father.

John's father reacted harshly, feeling that the family name had been disgraced, even by such odd circumstances. He demanded that his son return and give himself up to authorities. A younger brother, however, came to the rescue. This young man talked to the army authorities and enlisted in John's place in Napoleon's armed forces.

The custom of sending an alternate to battle was quite popular then. Finding people to serve in the army in one's place was a common practice. People who needed the money agreed to serve in the name of another person.

John went back to the seminary, relieved that he was being allowed to finish his studies for the priesthood, and grateful to his younger brother. Many young men of that era wanted to serve in the army, believing they would see the world and have an adventure.

Back in the seminary, John Vianney's Latin was still so bad that he had to learn philosophy and other subjects in French. Since Latin was the official language of the Church, he had to pass an examination in order to be ordained, and that was a problem. He failed the first test, then squeaked past the second with the help of friends. John Vianney was ordained in August, 1815.

Later, when some priests and Catholic lay people became envious of John Vianney, they wrote a petition demanding that his ordination to the priesthood be revoked (recalled). A friend showed him the petition, and John Vianney signed it, stating that the accusations saying that he was a slow learner were true. When the local bishop received the petition and found John Vianney's own signature at the bottom of the page, he laughed out loud and dismissed it as "sour grapes."

Despite the opposition and problems, John Vianney, newly ordained, was assigned to a parish under the control of one of his early patrons. This patron, and others like him, recognized the signs of John's holiness and went out of their way to keep others from harming him. After serving as an assistant pastor in the patron's parish for about three years, he was sent to Ars, another town near Lyon, in 1818.

There he settled in and started preaching and hearing confessions. He also opened an orphanage for poor girls, but the general lack of enthusiasm for the project in the parish made him give it up. His first rather astounding ability that marked his career was demonstrated at that time. The Curé of Ars was able to raise funds for programs in an almost miraculous fashion.

Although Ars was not very large, and John was a priest who could barely read and speak in Latin, large numbers of people began to arrive at the parish during the first months of his pastorate there. The reason was very simple: this was a man who could read hearts and souls. He also managed to convince many people to live decent God-fearing lives as a result of their meetings with him.

Imagine going into the confessional and rattling off past sins, then hearing the priest announce that the sins just confessed were not entirely true! Imagine the priest then listing one's actual sins, telling when and where they were committed.

Stunned, most people experiencing these revelations from the Curé of Ars believed that God had sent the priest to lead sinners back to the straight and narrow path. Even the most sophisticated person has second thoughts after hearing the truth come from the shadows of the confessional.

This was the second sign of the Curé of Ars's holiness. He could read the past and the future, and knew when men and women were trying to bluff him about their true spiritual condition. He had a keen insight as well, combined with a lot of common sense and an obvious connection with God and the secrets of human hearts.

Within two years of being appointed Curé of Ars he had attracted so many people that John Vianney was forced to sit in the confessional 16 to 18 hours a day. By 1855, as many as 20,000 men and women went to Ars each year to stand in line and make their confessions to the Curé. Bishops, priests, officials, the sick, and the sinful from everywhere arrived and waited their turn to hear him tell the truth and to advise them on what they should be doing for God and their own salvation.

The local bishop told the Curé of Ars not to take time off to make a retreat with the other clergymen of the region. In most dioceses of the world, retreats are held each year to educate the priests and to train them further in their duties. It is normally a time of spiritual renewal for these men.

But if the Curé was absent from the parish church of Ars, too many souls would be left unconsoled, without a helping hand. The bishop knew that people who had traveled long distances over bad roads would be upset that the Curé was gone when they needed him. The French had just experienced a terrible revolution, and had no hesitation about killing the clergy, especially bishops. The whole countryside would be better off if the Curé stayed at his post.

It was obvious to the bishop and others that John Vianney didn't need to learn how to become a Friend of God on a retreat. The sermons and lectures given to other priests wouldn't teach John Vianney anything that he didn't know already!

Then the sick began arriving in Ars, especially desperately ill French children, carried in the arms of their parents. People discovered that the Curé of Ars could heal them, bringing back health and happiness. This was the third mark of John Vianney's holiness.

The demands of the pilgrims were so great that a priest and a nun became John's helpers, and organizations were started to take care of the crowds arriving in the village. By this time the Curé's own health was failing fast. The many hours spent in the narrow space of the confessional, listening to people speak of their loneliness, pain, and weakness took their toll. The Curé lost his voice first. He then had to whisper his wisdom to his penitents during the last months, but somehow they heard him clearly.

When the Curé of Ars died on the 4th of August, 1859, word spread across Europe and people mourned their sad loss. He was canonized in 1925, and in 1929 was named the patron of parish priests by Pope Pius XI. John-Baptist-Marie Vianney's feast day is August 4th.

Zita

Chapter 21

Zita

This saint, also called Sitha or Citha, was born in 1218 in a village near Lucca, in the Tuscany region of Italy. The last name of the family is not listed in records, probably because they were people who were not considered important. Her family was noted for its piety (being deeply religious), since her older sister was a nun and her uncle was a saintly hermit. Zita, however, wasn't interested in convent life, or perhaps she was never asked by anyone to enter the sisterhood. Zita had been chosen for a different kind of service to God.

At the age of 12 she became a servant in the household of a wealthy merchant named Pagano di Fatinelli in the town of Lucca. Even at that young age, Zita served the household with care, impressing the other servants with her loyalty and generosity. In time Zita also impressed the members of the Fatinelli family, because she was one of the most divinely favored human beings ever.

Almighty God often blesses the simple, lowly-born people of the world, showing us that money, power, or even a good education doesn't matter when compared with truth, honor, courage, and loyalty to the faith. Some of the greatest popes in history, for example, came from poor farm towns, bringing with them the wisdom and holiness.

Zita worried about the sick and poor throughout her life, showing signs of this concern early. She spent her free time caring for them, and eventually she spent some of her working time tending to the long lines of the poor who started coming to her door. This enthusiasm caused upset in the Fatinelli household. If Zita had not been a Friend of God, chosen by him for a very special role, things might have turned out differently. The Fatinellis would have thrown her out for neglecting her duties.

Almighty God stepped in to make things right when Zita was busy caring for the suffering of the town. For example, when called away from baking bread in the kitchen one day, Zita went to the door to take care of a sick person. Other servants ran to the Fatinelli family to tell on Zita. As a result, servants and members of the family went to the kitchen to see for themselves. Entering the kitchen, they saw strange beings baking bread in the maidservant's place. These beings were not little green men from Mars! Their radiance, beauty, and spiritual power quickly made them known to everyone. Angels had come to perform Zita's tasks while she wrapped wounds and fed sick children. No one is going to toss a friend of angels out the door! The family members and the others servants gulped, prayed for forgiveness, and continued to support Zita's activities.

The needs for Zita's help was great. Lucca and other towns in the region were struck by a terrible famine, and Zita, unable to watch the suffering, gave away the family's entire supply of beans to the beggars at the door, which drew even more beggars to her door. When word spread of her goodness and kindness, the poor and needy made their way across the countryside to beg from Zita. She gave away the family's supply of beans because she saw people starving to death on her doorstep. The master of the household, old Pagano, who suspected what Zita had done, called her into his office and asked her to show him that his stock of food was safe and sound.

Zita was a bit alarmed over the request. She opened the cupboard, expecting to be beaten and fired for what she had done to the family, but the master seemed content. Looking into the cupboard herself, Zita saw that the beans had been replaced by God.

For 48 years Zita served the Fatinelli family and the people of Lucca. As she grew older the family excused her from regular duties and allowed her to take care of her beloved poor without any other worries. What did they have to lose? Angels baked their bread, beans were restored to their rightful places, and everyone felt better about life because Zita was with them.

Once on a Christmas Eve, she was loaned a fine cloak by her master, as Pagano didn't want her to go out into the cold without warm covering. Zita, naturally, gave it to a poor old man at the doorway of the local parish, Saint Frediano's. The old man said he knew that she was only loaning him the cloak, and he was grateful. When Zita returned home without it, Pagano went crazy with anger because Zita had pushed him too far. But while he was ranting and raving, Pagano was interrupted by the arrival of the old man at his door. The man had come to return the cloak with gratitude and blessings.

When word of this incident spread throughout Lucca, as stories do, people in the town began to speak of the old man as an angel. As a result, the parish doorway where the old man had received the cloak was renamed "the Angel Portal." It is called that today.

Zita died at the age of 60, on April 27, 1278, worn out from her care for the poor and sick. She was buried with all the honors the town of Lucca could give her, and she was canonized 400 years after her death. Her feast day is April 27th. She is patroness of housekeepers and maids, and she is also the one to ask for help in finding lost keys.

O Christ, thy guilty people spare,
So, bending at thy gracious throne,
Thy Virgin Mother pours her prayer,
Imploring pardon for her own. . .
Ye prophets and Apostles high
Behold our penitential tears,
And plead for us when death is nigh
And our all-searching Judge appears.
Ye Martyrs all, a purple band,
And Confessors, a white-robed train,
Oh, call us to our native land,
From this our exile back again.
And ye, O choir of Virgins chaste,
Receive us to your seats on high,
And hermits whom the desert waste
Sent up of old into the sky,
Drive from the flock, O spirits blest,
The false and faithless race away,
That all within one fold may rest
Secure beneath one Shepherd's sway.

Placare Christe Servius
Feast of All Saints